The Great Famine

John Gibney (ed.)

D1471762

PEN & SWORD
HISTORY

AN IMPRINT OF PEN & SWORD BOOKS LTD.
YORKSHIRE - PHILADELPHIA

First published in Great Britain in 2018 by
Pen & Sword History
An imprint of
Pen & Sword Books Ltd
Yorkshire - Philadelphia

Produced in association with History Ireland: www.historyireland.com

ISBN 9781526736635

Typeset in INDIA By Geniies IT & Services Private Limited.

Printed and bound in the UK by TJ International Ltd.

Pen & Sword Books Ltd incorporates the Imprints of Pen & Sword Books
Archaeology, Atlas, Aviation, Battleground, Discovery, Family History,
History, Maritime, Military, Naval, Politics, Railways, Select, Transport, True
Crime, Fiction, Frontline Books, Leo Cooper, Praetorian Press, Seaforth
Publishing, Wharncliffe and White Owl.

For a complete list of Pen & Sword titles please contact

PEN & SWORD BOOKS LIMITED
47 Church Street, Barnsley, South Yorkshire, S70 2AS, England
E-mail: enquiries@pen-and-sword.co.uk
Website: www.pen-and-sword.co.uk

or

PEN AND SWORD BOOKS
1950 Lawrence Rd, Havertown, PA 19083, USA
E-mail: Uspen-and-sword@casematepublishers.com
Website: www.penandswordbooks.com

Contents

Preface

The Irish potato famine of the 1840s - the 'Great Famine' or *An gorta mór* - is one of the defining events in modern Irish history. Over a five-year period a population of 8.2 million was reduced to 6.5 million through starvation, disease and emigration. The famine permanently changed one of the constituent parts of the United Kingdom as it then stood and its legacies - depopulation, socio-economic and cultural change, political resentment, and the expansion through mass emigration of an Irish 'diaspora' in Britain, North America and the British Empire - still have a resonance today. Now, in the first instalment of a new collaboration between Pen and Sword and *History Ireland* magazine, some of the world's leading experts on the Great Famine explore the crisis from a range of perspectives. From the importance of the potato in Irish history, to food exports, political change, the provision of charity, the impact of disease, the role of the authorities, the experience of emigration and the changing interpretation of the famine, this volume explores how this seminal event in Irish, British, and world history still has a relevance to the globalised world of the twenty-first century.

The chapters below have all been drawn from the archives of *History Ireland*, and re-edited; with regards to illustrations, every effort has been made to contact rights holders. If we have missed any, the error will be rectified in any subsequent edition.

Contributors

L. A. Clarkson is Emeritus Professor of Social History, Queen's University, Belfast.

E. Margaret Crawford was formerly Senior Research Fellow, Centre for Social Research, Queen's University, Belfast.

James S. Donnelly Jnr is Emeritus Professor of History at the University of Wisconsin-Madison.

Laurence M. Geary is Senior Lecturer in History at University College Cork.

John Gibney is a historian with the Royal Irish Academy's Documents on Irish Foreign Policy project.

Rob Goodbody is a geography and planner based in Dublin.

Peter Gray is Professor of Modern Irish History at Queen's University Belfast.

Timothy W. Guinnane is Philip Golden Bartlett Professor of Economic History at Yale University.

Christine Kinealy is Professor of History and founding director of Ireland's Great Hunger Institute at Quinnipiac University, Connecticut.

W. J. Lowe is Professor of History at Indiana University Northwest.

Trevor McClaughlin is Emeritus Professor in History at Macquarie University, Sydney, Australia.

Cormac Ó Gráda is Emeritus Professor of Economics at University College Dublin.

Michael Quigley was formerly historian for the lobby group Action Grosse Île.

Brian Walker is Emeritus Professor of Politics at Queen's University Belfast.

Introduction

Ireland's Great Famine

John Gibney

he Irish potato famine of the 1840s the Great Famine, (or in Irish, *an gorta mór*, literally 'the great hunger') is arguably the single most important event in modern Irish history prior to the achievement of independence from Britain in the 1920s. The impact of the famine is easily illustrated by its stark, mind-boggling statistics. The Irish population dropped from 8.2 million in 1841 to 6.5 million in 1851. Within that decline, 1,000,000 are assumed to have been killed by disease and starvation, with emigration accounting for the remainder. When one factors in a collapse in the birth rate of 3-400,000 as the population stopped growing, along with mass emigration, by 1851 the Irish population was perhaps 2,000,000 lower than it should have been: a demographic impact that has never been reversed, and probably never will be. In 1845 2.4 million acres were devoted to growing potatoes in Ireland; by 1847, thanks to the ravages of *phtophtera infestens* - the 'blight' that had so devastated potato crops - that number had collapsed to 284,000. The realities behind such figures make the famine the seminal event in modern Irish history. In the aftermath of the famine Ireland's population would continue to drop, emigration (especially to North America) became a permanent fixture in the worldview of generations of Irish people, the decline of the Irish language would accelerate, and Irish society and economy would be permanently altered. The fact that this could happen in the United Kingdom - then perhaps one of the wealthiest and advanced economies in the world - caused generations of Irish nationalists to hold up the famine as as exemplar of British misrule, and in its most extreme formulation, to use it as proof of a deliberate British plan to exterminate the Irish people.

The country that was devastated by the famine of the 1840s was an overwhelmingly rural society that was undergoing rapid change. Having been ruled by the British for centuries, since 1801 Ireland had been formally part of the United Kingdom. In political terms, Ireland had been formally ruled by a Protestant landed elite - the descendents of the British conquerers and colonists of the early modern era - but the 1820s had witnessed the mobilisation of Irish Catholics under the leadership of Daniel O'Connell in campaigns to remove the last lingering 'penal' restrictions on Catholic involvement in public life, and also in pursuit of repealing the Act of Union itself. With regards to socio-economic matters, since the 1820s Ireland had formed part of a free trade zone with Britain; this had made key Irish industries such as textiles vulnerable to British competition. When combined with the economic downturn that followed the end of the Napoleonic Wars in 1815, this ensured that the Irish economy in the first half of the nineteenth century was not in the rudest of health, though the Irish population continued to grow dramatically in this era. Ireland remained a predominantly rural society, and at the top of Ireland's complex and multi-layered system of landowning was the Protestant landed gentry. At the bottom of this social pyramid were the landless labourers known as 'cottiers', who often rented a small subsistence plot from landlords or farmers, usually in exchange for their labour rather than monetary payments. These, and the impoverished small farmers just above them on the lower rungs of the social ladder of rural Ireland, were the people most dependent on the potato.

The potato itself was a remarkably complete foodstuff that seems to have been introduced to Ireland in the late sixteenth century. By the end of the eighteenth century it had become a staple of Irish life, as Ireland's damp climate and acidic soil (especially in the western half of the country) offered perfect conditions for its widespread cultivation. The fact that it could grow in relatively poor soil

1. *The Potato Digger* by Paul Henry. (Ulster Museum)

also helped, and its expanding cultivation dovetailed with a rapidly expanding population from the late eighteenth century onwards (though whether this was a cause or a consequence of the rapid population growth of pre-famine Ireland is unclear). The potato was a valuable source of carbohydrates, proteins, and vitamins B and C. When combined with dairy products, it made for a nutritious (if unvaried) diet, and over time replaced dairy and pulses in the diet of the rural poor. It was also valuable as fodder, and prior to the famine one-third of Irish agricultural output was devoted to potato tillage.

No other European population depended on the potato to the degree that the Irish did. The consequence, in the 1840s, was arguably the worst humanitarian disaster of nineteenth-century Europe. The blight that devastated the potato crops came from South America, and was observed in Belgium in June 1845. It had reached Dublin by August 1845 and was observed nationwide by early September. The 'blight' devastated potato crops in Ireland in 1845 with frightening rapidity. The impact of the blight was not confined to Ireland: potato crops were devastated across the continent in the mid-1840s, but no segment of the population of any other European country depended upon the potato to the extent that the Irish poor did; the consequences were disastrous, as famine was the result. There had been periods of dearth due to poor potato harvests in the 1820s and 1830s, but this was different. In 1845 perhaps a third to a fourth of the crop failed, prompting emergency relief measures by Sir Robert Peel's Tory Government, who ordered the surreptitious purchase of maize in North America and the opening of food depots along the west coast. The partial failure of 1845 was followed by a major failure of the potato crop in 1846. The spores of the fungus had been washed into the ground in the course of the wet winter of 1845-46, to re-emerge the following summer. This major crop failure saw the first reports of fatalities, and relief works began; the 130 workhouses established under the poor law of 1838 were under pressure by the end of the year. The public institutions that existed in Ireland (such as dispensaries) were never designed to cope with this crisis with which they were now faced.

Official relief measures did have an impact: by the end of 1847 700,000 were employed on public works, with soup kitchens feeding huge numbers between January and October 1847. But despite the obvious effectiveness of the soup kitchens, they were phased out, and the burden of relief was shifted onto the Irish poor law by the new Whig-Liberal Government of Sir John Russell. Irish resources were to pay for what was deemed to be an Irish problem, despite the fact that Ireland was a part of the United Kingdom, and public works were to justify the administration of relief. There were limits to official charity. Senior treasury officials such as Charles Trevalyan argued that the famine was the unavoidable consequence of various Irish social evils, which needed to be urgently reformed (and racist and sectarian attitites can undoubtedly be seen in some British responses to the famine). On a more basic level, the view of

2. Sir Walter Raleigh – did he really introduce the potato to Ireland? (National Gallery of Ireland)

the British Government was that the relief of the famine was a responsibility that should fall upon the shoulders of Irish landlords, as they were responsible for the plight of their tenants. While some landlords behaved responsibly and humanely, others – and many strong farmers – used the famine as a pretext for

3. Sir Francis Drake – 'introducer of the potato into Europe, in the year of
Our Lord 1580' according to a monument in Offenburg, Germany. (National
Portrait Gallery, London)

4. *Herbal* contained the first illustration of a potato ever published.

widespread evictions, or profiteered from the crisis. It was cheaper to evict ten-ants than to maintain them.

On the whole, the official reaction to the crisis in Ireland was inadequate. Private charity went some way towards plugging the gap. As noted by Rob Goodbody, organised charity drives across the UK and North America helped to alleviate, to some degree, the desperate human reality of the famine. A

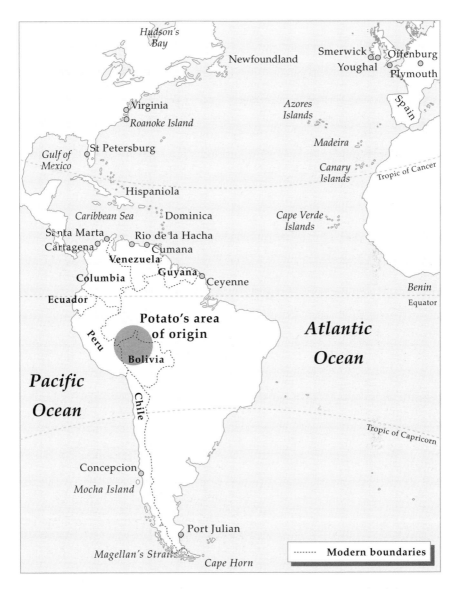

5. Map showing the more temperate areas of the potato's area of origin.

harrowing account of a visit to Belmullet in Mayo—the county most badly ravaged by the famine—was left by the English Quaker William Bennett:

'The scenes of human misery and degradation we witnessed will haunt my imagination, with the vividness and power of some horrid and tyrannous delusion, rather than the features of a sober reality...perhaps the poor children presented the most piteous and heart-rending spectacle. Many were too weak to stand, their little limbs attenuated—except when the frightful swellings had taken the place of previous emaciation—beyond the *power of volition when moved*. Every infantile expression entirely departed; and in some, reason and intelligence had evidently flown. Many were *remnants of families*, crowded together in one cabin; orphaned little relatives taken in by the equally destitute, and even strangers...they did but rarely complain. When inquired of what was the matter, the answer was alike in all—"*Tha shein ukrosh*"—*indeed the hunger*. We truly learned the terrible meaning of that sad word, *ukrosh*.'

While deaths from starvation were widespread, malnutrition opened the door to diseases such as typhus, dysentery, and cholera. The precise death toll from the famine was almost certainly higher than that suggested by the 1851 census, on which details of deaths outside the public institutions were to be recorded by family members. But what if an entire family was dead, or had emigrated?

The Great Famine could be said to have burned itself out; many historians post 1852 as the year in which it could definitively be said to have ended. The highest death rates during the famine were to be found in the south and the west: the areas that also saw the highest confirmed deaths from outright starvation. The impact of the famine mirrored the east-west divide between a relatively literate, Anglophone, mixed economy and a largely illiterate, Irish–speaking agricultural region. The western half of the country had the worst dwellings, lowest rates of literacy, and the highest proportion of people employed in agriculture; areas with more mixed economies, such as the north-east, were better equipped to deal with the crisis. But the sheer scale of the Great Famine had a profound and irreversible effect on Irish society. Nowhere was left untouched, and it had more obvious long-term implications. The famine triggered Irish emigration on a mass scale. It accelerated the decline and dispersal overseas of the Irish language, and the erosion of the rich vernacular culture that the language had encapsulated. Farmers in the post-famine era shifted towards livestock cultivation, which ensured that, on the one hand, land became scarcer, and this tightening of opportunities at home fed the ongoing emigrant stream to the new Irish communities being established overseas; while on the other hand, it helped the creation of the new rural and urban Catholic middle-classes who would become the new dominant elites of pre-independence Ireland, at least outside Ulster. And this is to say nothing of lingering resentments that found political expression. The changes wrought by the famine were profound and varied; suffice to say, the creation of modern Ireland can largely be dated to the 1840s. The chapters that follow, all of which have been re-edited from their original publication, probe some of the ways in which the basis for those changes were laid.

Chapter 1

A non-famine history of Ireland?

L.A. Clarkson and E. Margaret Crawford

I s it possible to write famine out of Irish history? Note, the question refers to 'famine', not the 'Great Famine'. The catastrophe of 1845-49 was unlike any previous famine. In the words of Peter Solar it 'was no ordinary subsistence crisis'. Its singularity notwithstanding, Ireland's story is often told with famine as a fugue running through a dolorous past. Yet we have concluded that Ireland was not a hunger-prone country, or at least not more hunger-prone than other European countries. The people of Ireland were not born to famine, although, along with their neighbours, they endured the pain of hunger whenever the harvests failed.

Until the late eighteenth century, and even into the early nineteenth, the history of Western Europe was punctuated by subsistence crises that sometimes erupted into full-scale hunger. From the great famine that ravaged Northern Europe in the early fourteenth century to the crisis of 1816-17, the poor in Europe endured famished years during which some people starved to death, and many more died from infections and deficiency diseases. Most famines were caused by failures of the grain crops brought on by bad weather. Shortages were exacerbated by an uneven distribution of food with some people enjoying plenty while others starved. Ireland shared the sufferings of Western Europe, to a greater or lesser extent. At the turn of the sixteenth and seventeenth centuries and again in the 1650s, the devastations of war added to the anguish. But Ireland was not unique in this respect. Armies in Europe could be just as devastating. Germany, for example, lost possibly 40 per cent of its population during the Thirty Years War, most of it to hunger and disease. There were, of course, many famine-free years and in the years between famines there was enough food in Ireland to satisfy everybody. This is not a notion that fits comfortably into the conventional story. Yet for much of her history, people in Ireland had plenty to eat. The rich ate more lavishly than the poor, but so did they everywhere. Overindulgence was not a sin peculiar to the Irish upper classes.

Ireland is naturally endowed to be a pastoral society. Before extensive settlement from England and Scotland in the later sixteenth century the diet of the people contained plenty of meat, butter and milk. But as English military commanders understood all too well, grain was an important component of winter

6. Irish beggars *c*.1840—note the basket of potatoes. (National Library of Ireland)

7. Relief works, Inverin Hill, County Galway, *c.*1890 – during the Famine the money earned from such schemes was not enough. (Sean Sexton)

food supplies. As colonisation progressed, the boundaries of cultivation were pushed further outwards. The growth of total food production cannot be measured directly, but it was expanding sufficiently to support a burgeoning export trade and feed the growing population at home. Through the seventeenth and early eighteenth centuries food exports consisted mainly of barreled beef, pork and butter, but after 1750 Ireland became also a major exporter of grain. There is no evidence that consumers in Ireland went chronically hungry to meet the demands of overseas markets. As long as the harvests did not fail or the livestock succumb to fatal disease, there was plenty of food available to all those who had legal access to it, an important proviso to which we will return.

From the mid-eighteenth century potatoes became important in diets. They had been cultivated in Ulster since the early seventeenth century and by the end of the century they were commonplace in the gardens of the peasantry: 'their dearly beloved potatoes' in the words of John Dunton. In the next century potatoes were incorporated into agricultural rotations, as a clearing crop on ground newly dug for the cultivation of corn. Potatoes enabled the margins of cultivation to be pushed further and further into the mild, damp West. Cultivators turned the virgin soil with spades and dug in dung scraped from byres and farmyards. Then they planted potatoes in the so-called lazy beds. After the potatoes were lifted the land was ready for a crop of corn. Land, labour and

8. Pigs were potatoes capitalised: they were fattened on potatoes and sold for the money needed to pay the rent and the few articles of clothing and furniture essential for life. (Sean Sexton)

capital were thus brought together in an economical fashion. Crucially, potatoes added to the food supply. They fed humans and pigs alike. For a 100 years the population of Ireland grew more rapidly than elsewhere in Western Europe, sustained by a plant that was abundant and nourishing.

Abundance and nutritional value are the essential characteristics of potatoes, to which we should add cheapness and convenience. Potatoes were easy to cook and to eat: a turf fire, a cooking pot, and fingers were all that were required. As long as potatoes flourished, they banished famine from the land. Within the context of Irish history potatoes have been cast in the role of the great saviour, the crop that kept the Malthusian spectre at bay. Alternatively, potatoes have sometimes been seen as having been inflicted on the native population by an iniquitous land system.

Potatoes contain good quality protein (unusual for a vegetable) and, if eaten in sufficient quantities, provide enough energy and vitamin C to sustain good health. Potatoes and milk together constitute a nutritious diet, albeit a rather monotonous one. Potatoes yielded abundantly: six tons or more per acre in a normal year in the eighteenth century. This was enough to keep a labourer, his wife and children—and his pig—well fed for much of the year. Only the 'meal

9. Blight-affected potatoes preserved for posterity. (Bord Fáilte)

10. 'Irish Lord feasting: the Feast of the MacSwynes' from John Derricke's *The Image of Irelande* (1581) – for much of her history, people in Ireland had plenty to eat.

months' during the summer, before the new crop was ready, were a problem, but then oatmeal and herrings were generally at hand to fill the gap.

People ate potatoes for pleasure. 'Mark the Irishman's potato bowl placed on the floor', wrote Arthur Young, 'the whole family on their hams around it, devouring a quantity almost incredible, the beggar seating himself to it with a hearty welcome, the pig taking his share as readily as the wife, the cocks, hens, turkeys, geese, the cur, the cat, and perhaps the cow—and all partaking out of the same dish. No man can often have been a witness of it without being convinced of the plenty, and I will add, the cheerfulness that attends it'. Not only the poor cottage dwellers, but also well-bred ladies enjoyed potatoes. In 1775 they formed 'a standing dish at every meal; these are eaten by way of bread, even by the ladies indelicately placing them on the table-cloth, on the side of the plate, after peeling them. By the 1820s 'a partiality [for potatoes] is entertained by every intermediate rank to the palace, no table being without them'.

But it was poverty more than pleasure that pushed one third of the population onto potatoes to the exclusion of almost everything else by the beginning of the nineteenth century. A combination of the agrarian structures and economic circumstances created this precarious dependence. Most land in the eighteenth century was owned by landlords who farmed it out to subordinate landlords (the middlemen of popular infamy) or to tenant farmers. They, in turn, sub-let land to cottier-labourers. As the population multiplied, tens of thousands of very small holdings were created. From about 1750 much of the land was used to grow wheat, oats, and barley, a good deal of which was exported. But labourers and small landholders—the groups were virtually indistinguishable—tilled tiny plots to grow potatoes. The potato patches provided cheap food that served as the economic base for marriage. By the end of the eighteenth century marriage was the almost universal condition for Irish men and women. They did not marry particularly young—normally in their early twenties—but that so many young men and women entered the matrimonial state contributed to a high level of general fertility. Potatoes kept husbands and wives and their children healthy. More speculatively, mashed potatoes and milk made a convenient weaning food, enabling babies to be taken from the breast at an early age. Thus, young mothers lost the contraceptive benefits of extended lactation; and so marital fertility as well as general fertility was high in the century before the Great Famine.

Potatoes and people formed a fertile alliance. The toil of the cottiers prepared the lazy beds and planted the potatoes. Potatoes fed them and kept them healthy and breeding. What benefit did the farmers derive from sub-division? They gained a supply of cheap labour which raised the crops that fed the better off and made Ireland an important exporter of food.

By the beginning of the nineteenth century men labouring in the fields consumed the equivalent of ten to fourteen pounds of raw potatoes a day, washed down with milk or buttermilk. Their wives and children ate less in proportion and the family pig demolished a similar amount. Pigs were potatoes capitalised: they were fattened on potatoes and sold for the money needed to pay the rent and the few articles of clothing and furniture essential for life. But how was it that the poor came to rely so much on a single source of food? Part of the answer is that potatoes were cheap, plentiful, nourishing, and convenient. Everything else was sent to market. As Robert Bell explained in 1804, '[the peasantry] lived on those things for which little or no money could be procured at market: potatoes constituted their chief food. The next article he retained for his own use was one of still less value, it was that part of the milk which remained behind after butter had been extracted from it'.

Potatoes entered diets too late for their failure to play a significant part in famines before the mid-eighteenth century. During the famine of 1727-28 potatoes eased the blow of the failure of the grain harvests. In the severe famine of 1740-41 the cereal harvests were poor and the potato crop was ruined by the great frost in the winter of 1739-40. By now a significant proportion of the population relied on potatoes for their winter food and their loss created severe hardship. As many as 480,000 people may have starved to death or died of famine-related diseases in 1740 and 1741, a mortality rate (if accurate) proportionately greater than during the Great Famine.

Nothing so terrible occurred again for a 100 years. There were periodic shortages of food as the grain or potato harvests failed as the result of cold or wet. The years 1783-84 were especially bad, but the hardships of the second half of the eighteenth century were localised and short-lived. At the end of the century bad weather, harvest failures, and wartime inflation made 1799 and 1800 very difficult for the poor. In 1816-17 famine deaths may have reached 80,000. Harvests were poor throughout Europe as dust from volcanic eruptions in the East Indies blotted out the sun and resulted in two cold years. Ireland, though, was less badly affected than continental Europe. Further localised food shortages occurred in 1822 and in the early 1830s, but it is only with a very large dose of hindsight that these episodes can be interpreted as ineluctable steps to the Great Famine.

During the Great Famine the potato crops failed from an unknown cause. Previous failures of cereals and potato were the result of bad weather. Occasionally the growth of potatoes was curtailed by drought. Leaf curl and rot depressed yields in one or two years. Nothing, though, portended the arrival of *phytophthora infestans.* The disease had first been seen in North America in 1843 and was spotted in Belgium in June 1845. Its arrival in Ireland was famously announced in the *Gardeners' Chronicle* in September 1845. One or two observers identified the blight as a fungal infestation, but government officials, scientists, landlords, and cultivators alike were united in not knowing how to deal with it.

Phytophthora infestans was an omnivorous destroyer of potatoes. A third of the harvest was lost in the first year (1845), 75 per cent in the second year, and 37 per cent in the fourth year. Yields in the third year ('Black '47') were normal, but little had been planted. Losses of this extent and sustained over four years were, as Peter Solar has pointed out, way beyond anything that could be predicted based on European experience. The intensity of the failures was magnified because three million people relied on potatoes for their survival. Potatoes rotted elsewhere in the United Kingdom and in Europe in 1845-49, but it was only in Ireland that they were almost the sole support of so many people. Their loss left people starving and vulnerable to deficiency diseases, and infections such as typhus, relapsing fever, diarrhoea and dysentery. Infections themselves are not the direct consequence of chronic hunger, but malnutrition lowers peoples' resistance to infections; and the towns and feeding stations into which the starving people crowded were havens for infectious diseases of all kinds.

The death of 12 per cent of the population between 1845 and 1851 as a result of famine did not quite reach the proportion suffered in 1740-41, but the absolute number—approximately 1,000,000 dead—was beyond past experience. This was all the more shocking because it happened so late into the nineteenth century. To the deaths of the born we must add the unborn, that is births that might have occurred had the famine not killed the potential parents.

These averted births could have totalled 400,000. Another one million people fled Ireland. In a few short years Ireland lost two million men, women, and children.

What could have been done to avert such a tragedy? This question more than any other has dominated considerations of the Great Famine and the answers have done much to force famine to the forefront of Irish history. Over the course of the Great Famine the supply of calories declined by almost a quarter. At the same time there was a reduction in the amount of grain (mainly oats) exported. There was also a fall in the quantities of cereals and potatoes used for brewing and distilling and fewer potatoes went to feed pigs. Indian corn was imported from America to offset the loss of the potatoes. But the fact remains that the blight deprived the poor of their basic food. Peter Solar has argued that the loss of potatoes between 1845 and 1849 was so great that the gap was too large to be plugged.

The fungus did not attack wheat, barley or oats, although poor weather and a shortage of labour depressed their output. Nor was the production of meat (apart from pork and bacon) and butter seriously disrupted. Many people have argued, therefore, that there was enough food available to feed the hungry and prevent starvation. The loss of potatoes might not have been entirely compensated for by giving the poor access to the corn, meat, butter, and beer that were exported. But the diversion of exports to domestic consumption might have saved many lives.

This diversion, though, was not a simple matter. Individuals—farmers and merchants—owned the exports and they were engaged in normal market trading. Presumably they would have sold their grain, meat and butter in Ireland had it been profitable to do so. But the poor did not have the money to buy the food. In the language of Amartya Sen, they lacked 'entitlements' because they did not own it and could not afford to purchase it. The alternatives were that somebody else—benevolent landlords, the clergy, or the government, perhaps—should buy it for them, or that the poor should be provided with work so that they could earn the money.

Some landlords did spend money feeding the poor, Catholic priests and Protestant clergy did what they could, but many landlords were not in a position to help or were unwilling to do so. For the government the issue was one of cost and attitudes. The money would have to come from the Treasury or from local rates. The will was lacking in Westminster to sanction massive spending and Irish ratepayers were reluctant to pay higher taxes. In all the government spent £9.5 million on famine relief, including the soup kitchens that functioned through the spring and early summer of 1847. This was a measly amount in face of a huge disaster.

Work aid was tried in 1846 and 1847, but the schemes were widely criticised for their inefficiency. In any case the money earned was not enough. In March

1847 the journalist Alexander Somerville came across a man earning ten old pence a day. He met his wife and children, 'skeletons all of them, with skin on the bones and life within the skin'. The earnings were simply too little to make any difference. From the autumn of 1847 poor relief was left to the inadequate workhouses or to private charity. The government in Westminster had a touching faith in the market. To interfere with private property was anathema. Therefore relief food had to be purchased or, if distributed freely, it should go only to those people deemed to be deserving of it. However, market mechanisms were ill-suited to cure Ireland's problems. The potato eaters were poorly integrated into the market. They were frequently paid, not in money, but by the use of land on which to grow potatoes. For many of them their source of cash was the pig; but the pig too was a casualty of the famine. If they were able to find paid employment their wages were not enough to pay for the food they and their families needed. The market-based ideas of political economy prevalent in mid-nineteenth century Britain could not save the starving people of Ireland.

The Great Famine was a unique event that has dominated a great deal of Irish historiography. It has produced a teleological view in which everything that came before leads to the crisis. But we should avoid the conclusion that Irishmen, women and children in the past lived in a state of chronic under-nourishment, which not infrequently turned into full-scale starvation. In the sixteenth and seventeenth centuries there was meat aplenty: 'As for the greatest Karne, thei have the cheefest stuffe:\ Though dirtie tripes and offals like please under knaues enough.' So wrote John Derricke in 1581. In the early seventeenth century, according to Fynes Moryson, the 'mere Irish' drank milk straight from the cow, ate lumps of butter but no flesh except 'that which dies of disease or otherwise of itself, feed mostly on white meats [i.e. dairy produce], and esteem for a great dainty sour curds, vulgarly called by them Bonnaclabbe'. Sir William Petty reported in 1672 that during winter, the Irish ate 'bread in cakes'. In the summer, if they lived near the sea, people had shellfish harvested from the shoreline. For everybody there was the occasional hen or rabbit, all washed down with 'milk, sweet and sower, thick and thin'. They ate 'potatoes from August to May'. Potatoes became increasingly important as a winter food and by the end of the eighteenth century constituted the main food of the poor. They were tasty, cheap, abundant, nourishing, and convenient. For the poor they were a boon. They were too bulky in relation to value to be traded extensively, and they could not be stored from year to year. The danger of potatoes, though, lay less in themselves than in the dominant position they assumed in diets. If the harvests failed, as they did in 1845, 1846, and 1848, then the potato eaters were left precariously exposed.

It is possible to write a non-famine history of Ireland, but the story of Ireland with the Great Famine left out would make no sense.

Chapter 2

The lumper potato and the famine

Cormac Ó Gráda

Many contributions to pre-famine Irish economic history have drawn attention to the apparent contrast between the abject poverty of the Irish masses and their relatively high nutritional status. Poverty, they argue, was mitigated by a potato-dominated diet which, while monotonous, was adequate in terms of calories and protein. Modern nutritional analysis indeed concedes that potatoes are a remarkably complete foodstuff, one that can serve as virtually the sole component in a human diet. But this raises a question mark about the potato, since the potatoes consumed in pre-famine Ireland differ from those common today. The poor reputation of the kind most closely linked to the famine, the notorious 'Lumper', makes the question all the more apposite. Thus, in assessing calorie intake before the famine, knowing the acreage under potatoes and the average yield per acre is not enough: potato quality is also important.

In 1810 the Cork agriculturist Horatio Townsend noted that Irish potatoes were 'pleasant, mealy, and nourishing' compared to the 'watery and ill-flavoured' varieties prevalent in England. Potato quality declined in Ireland thereafter, however, and on the eve of the famine the very poor were often forced to rely almost exclusively on inferior varieties, notably the Lumper. Thus in 1832 a Kerry campaigner against tithes complained that '*gan do bhiadh againn ach lompers agus an nídh nach ar bfiudh leis na ministéirighe d'ithead* (our only food being lumpers and what the ministers would not eat)'. When the English radical William Cobbett visited Waterford in 1834, he was told that 'when men or women are employed, at six-pence a day and their board, to dig Minions or Apple-potatoes, they are not suffered to taste them, but are sent to another field to dig Lumpers to eat'.

For the poor, who evidently preferred the premium Apple potato and even the Cup (hardy but coarser than the Apple), the spread of the Lumper indicated impoverishment. It was tasteless, but was it also poor food? The dry matter content (i.e. starch) in any crop of potatoes is quite variable: climate, pests, soil and agricultural practices all play a role. Variety is also crucial and, given its poor press, the watery and ungainly Lumper probably contained less dry matter than other cultivated varieties. But did it also contain less than modern varieties?

And how widely was it consumed? We cannot assume that the nutritional quality of pre-famine foods matched that of modern varieties.

The crucial question remains less how the Lumper compared with the Apple, the Cup, or the Minion than how it would rate against modern dry matter estimates. When compared with contemporary supermarket varieties, the Lumper's weight loss from cooking, as reported in 1840 – two ounces in every

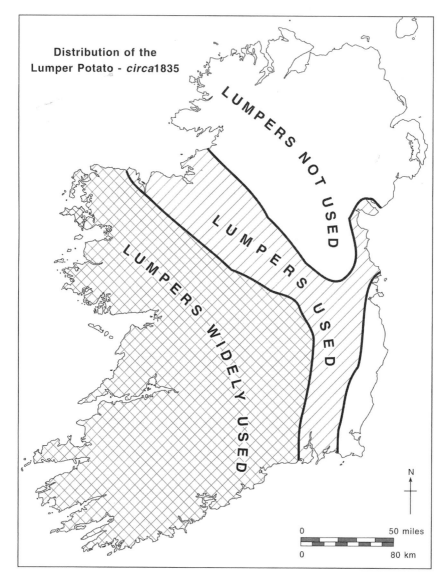

11. Distribution map of Lumper potato usage.

sixteen- was much greater. Thus a labourer's daily intake of potatoes before the Famine (estimated at between 10 and 14 lbs!) was in reality reduced by the time it was consumed at the dinner table. Royal Dublin Society tests in the 1830s of the actual weight (specific gravity) of potato varieties found that the Lumper was the lowest at 1.084. The higher the specific gravity the 'better' the potato: potatoes with a specific gravity of one would float in water! A standard conversion produces dry matter estimates of 28, 24 and 21 per cent for the Apple, Cup, and Lumper, respectively. On average, starch content works out at about 80 per cent of the dry matter content. From the statistics, the Lumper's lowly status is plain. Although the Lumper has not been commercially cultivated for a long time, it was still grown in some districts in the 1920s, and specimens survive in a few 'museum' collections in Ireland and Scotland (an enterprising farmer from County Antrim successfully bred it in 2013, and his crop was stocked by Marks & Spencer). The Scottish Agriculture and Fishery Department's scientific services in Edinburgh has a rich collection of such varieties. During 1991, officials there grew a range of modern and 'museum' varieties (including the Lumper), and measured their dry matter content and specific gravity. In this experiment, the Lumper performed poorly compared to premium varieties, either modern or 'museum', but quite well relative to modern supermarket varieties.

The Lumper was introduced to Ireland from Scotland in the 1800s. Before that, dozens of varieties were cultivated: in 1812 it was claimed that each county had its own favourite. The Lumper spread rapidly due to its higher yields, adaptability to poor soils, and (not least) reliability. It had made big inroads by the 1840s, but the common belief that the Irish relied on it almost exclusively on the eve of the famine must be qualified. Nearly all witnesses to the questionnaire in the Poor Inquiry of 1835-36 mentioned potatoes as the main item in the diet. Twenty-one witnesses (from a total of over 1,500) were more specific about the poor quality of potato consumed in their area. One referred to 'that most unhealthy of vegetables, the lumper potato', another to 'a bad description of potato called lumper', a third to 'the worst description of potato', and so on. Such remarks were regionally concentrated; Galway produced four of them, Mayo five, Laois three, Cork three, Carlow, Westmeath, Roscommon, Limerick, Kerry, Derry, and Tipperary one each. Moreover, the Tipperary reference was to 'some potatoes of the worst description called Connaught lumpers'. The sharp east-west gradient in the Lumper's distribution seems, therefore, to be significant. Another guide to its diffusion is found in the replies to the centenary inquiry into the famine in folk memory, carried out by the Irish Folklore Commission in 1945-46, which contain several mentions of varieties found before the famine. These accounts are not above suspicion, since they sometimes claim for the pre-famine era post-famine varieties no longer common or extinct by the 1940s. Moreover, some potato varieties – like some jigs and reels today – may well have been known by different names in different counties. The many names given included Green Tops, White Rocks, and American Sailors (Kerry), White Tops (Carlow), Skerry Blues, Red Scotch Downs or Peelers, and White Scotch Downs (Westmeath), Thistlewhippers and Pink Eyes (Cavan), Prodestans (Mayo), Weavers (Down), Leathers and Mingens (i.e. Minions) (Kerry), Cups, Buns, Millers' Thumbs, and Derry Bucks (Donegal), and Coipíní (or Cups) (Connemara). The Lumper was mentioned too, though not often. On the whole, the evidence suggests greater variety than allowed for by the historiography.

The Lumper is doubly notorious in Irish history, for being poor food in the decades leading up to the Great Famine, and for offering such poor resistance to *phytophthera infestans*. Fair enough. And yet, though the Lumper was definitely dull fare, it usually provided the requisite calories before 1845. Moreover, though most historians deem the cottiers who switched to the Lumper to have traded security for large crops, it was originally introduced from Scotland for both sturdiness and yield. Finally, the Lumper will always be linked to the Great Hunger by its dominance in Ireland by the 1840s: yet it should be remembered that all other varieties commonly sown at the time also succumbed to the blight.

Chapter 3

Punch and the Great Famine

Peter Gray

The widespread use of *Punch* cartoons in books and teaching materials on nineteenth century history is hardly surprising: these often striking images are a convenient visual aid for understanding a period in which photography was in its infancy. Yet the use of this graphic record in an unreflective manner is fraught with difficulties and may detract from the material's historical usefulness. Many have been guilty of this unimaginative use of sources, and consequently can be accused of having missed the point of the illustrations. The historical significance of *Punch* in the later 1840s lay as much in its aspiration and ability to mould public perceptions of events, as in its satiric commentaries on those events. The paper provided no direct record of the mass sufferings of the Irish peasantry (in contrast to the *Illustrated London News'* graphic depictions), but Irish affairs occupied many of its pages in the famine years. Perhaps its greatest importance to the historian is as a simultaneous shaper and expression of British public opinion – a phenomenon vital to our understanding of the famine as a whole.

Founded in 1841, *Punch* sought to establish a new style of humorous journalism, more tasteful and restrained than the savage caricatures of Gillray and Cruikshank, but also more serious and campaigning than its comic rivals. From the start, it had a moralistic cutting edge, derived from its radical founders, Henry Mayhew and Douglas Jerrold. Even its more conservative contributors believed that humour should be about more than mere laughter. The novelist William Makepeace Thackeray, a regular writer from 1843 to 1854, expressed the view that humour ought 'to awaken and direct your love, your pity, your kindness; your scorn of untruth, pretension, imposture; your tenderness for the weak, the poor, the oppressed, the unhappy'. This was indeed the mission of the early *Punch* which led philanthropic assaults on sweated labour, poor law abuses, and terrible urban conditions. The paper's radicalism was, however, distinctly middle-class in tone; while critical of Chartism, it threw itself whole-heartedly behind the free trade and financial reform movements. Already by the late 1840s, it was beginning a transition to the more complacent conservative stance it would adopt as a patriotic national institution in the mid-Victorian 'age of equipoise'. *Punch*'s political weight was considerable.

12. A parallel between Peel and Caesar. (*Punch*)

Its circulation, at around 30,000, was below that of many other journals and was largely concentrated in London, but it reached many metropolitan opinion-formers who set the tone of British middle-class attitudes as expressed nationally. It was read by politicians, and several cabinet ministers commented on its pronouncements in their private diaries. Most importantly, *Punch* existed as part of a network of similarly-oriented journals. Its authors were keen to take their line on public affairs largely from *The Times*, by far the most influential newspaper of the day. Indeed one contributor, Gilbert a Beckett, was simultaneously a leader writer for both *The Times* and the *Illustrated London News*. The power of these three papers taken together was considerable – each complemented the other by focusing on a different aspect of middle-class taste. This was all the more true in a period of party flux, weak governments, and a national radical middle-class mobilisation.

   Punch had a history of broad sympathy for the plight of Ireland, mixed with a mocking hostility towards the Irish political leader Daniel O'Connell and the movement to repeal the Act of Union. In the early stages of the famine catastrophe, O'Connell was attacked for his alleged greed in collecting the 'repeal rent' from the starving poor and for misleading his ignorant followers as to their real interests. ['The real potato blight of Ireland', 13 December 1845] Attention was thus directed away from the realities of the socio-economic crisis, to what were regarded in Britain as the ludicrous and seditious political antics of the Irish. Political and moral factors were to be relentlessly harped upon in the subsequent years as the true causes of Irish distress. While 'Hibernia' could be treated sympathetically as a feminized abstract, and her 'Haughty Sisters, Britannia and Caledonia' upbraided for their self-satisfied aloofness ['The Irish Cinderella', 25 April 1846], *Punch* regarded the famine more as an opportunity to 'conquer' Ireland 'by food and education', than as a case for simple charity.

ALFRED THE SMALL,

DISGUISED AS A LITTLE WARBLER, VISITING THE IRISH CAMP;

BEING A GRAND HISTORICAL PARODY UPON ALF—D THE GR—AT VISITING THE DANISH DITTO;

And Intended for a Presco in the New Houses of Parliament.

13. Alfred the Small. (*Punch*)

The excessive luxuries of the rich in Britain were a target more conducive to radical (and indeed evangelical) criticism than an inadequate relief policy.

The paper mocked the anti-Catholic interpretations of famine causation proposed by some evangelical Protestants, but it did not rule out the hand of God. Indeed it implicitly gave credence to providentialist views which saw the

THE BRITISH LION AND THE IRISH MONKEY.

Monkey (Mr. Mitchell). "One of us MUST be 'Put Down.'"

14. British lion and Irish monkey. (*Punch*)

potato blight as a means of replacing 'backward' potatoes (and the social system their cultivation supported) with more 'civilised' foodstuffs. It agreed with *The Times* that 'providence, which made us and the land we till, evidently intended another subsistence' than the potato, that 'most precarious of crops and meanest of foods'. Ministers agreed that the introduction of cheap imported grain would transform the Irish character. Edward Cardwell argued 'if, while they diffused among [the Irish] a taste for a higher kind of food, they could also introduce amongst them habits of industry and improvement calculated to furnish them with the means of procuring that higher food, they would be effecting one of the greatest practical improvements which this country was capable of accomplishing'.

This policy necessitated a strict adherence to free trade in food and bound up Ireland's fate with the repeal of the corn laws. From the autumn of 1846 British governments adopted a bi-partisan policy of minimal interference in the food trade. The collapse in the price of imported Indian meal the following summer appeared to vindicate this free trade dogma, but this was of little consolation to the hundreds of thousands who perished in the winter of 1846-47. The social costs of that year blunted but did not change the moralistic British critique of potato subsistence; *Punch* prematurely welcomed the apparent restoration of

CONSOLATION FOR THE MILLION.—THE LOAF AND THE POTATO.

15. Consolation for the million. (*Punch*)

the potato to health in autumn 1847 (it failed again in 1848 and 1849), but only as a subsidiary to cheap bread. ['Consolation for the million: The loaf and the potato', 11 September 1847] Like Sir Charles Trevelyan, the assistant Secretary to the Treasury, *Punch* regarded the continuation of famine conditions in Ireland after this time as entirely due to indigenous moral and not biological failures. Ireland had been warned of the folly of potato dependence by a 'natural' disaster, but had perversely chosen to ignore the danger; no further responsibility could be undertaken by the 'imperial' government.

   The relief of famine distress was bound up with ideological considerations. In the cartoon 'Union is strength' (17 October 1846), John Bull, the epitome of Englishness, presents his Irish 'brother' not only with food, but with a spade – to put him 'in a way to earn your own living'. In the light of modern conceptions of the importance of development aid, the offer appears sensible, but it must be understood in the light of the popularised versions of political economy current at the time. Thomas Campbell Foster's analysis of the 'Condition of the People of Ireland', serialised by *The Times* in 1845-46, had stressed the essential fertility of Ireland and placed the blame for its backwardness on ignorance and a lack of enterprise. The idea that wealth could be created by industrious exertion alone (capital being merely 'accumulated labour'

THE ENGLISH LABOURER'S BURDEN;

OR, THE IRISH OLD MAN OF THE MOUNTAIN.

[See *Sinbad the Sailor.*

16. English labourer's burden. (*Punch*)

considerable popularity. There was also a widespread belief, shared by some ministers, that Ireland possessed sufficient surplus in its 'wages-fund' to support its current population, if only this was diverted from landlord extravagance to productive use. While *Punch* acknowledged that the scale of the 1846-47 crisis necessitated some assistance, and rejected the crude Malthusianism of Lord Radnor, this feeling continued to lie at the root of its perceptions. With

THE NEW IRISH STILL.

SHOWING HOW ALL SORTS OF GOOD THINGS MAY BE OBTAINED (BY INDUSTRY) OUT OF PEAT.

17. New Irish still. (*Punch*)

The Times, it advocated the early introduction of a permanent extended Irish poor law, which would make Irish property support Irish poverty. This 'very bitter pill', strictly administered as a moral spur to self-reliance on the part of all Irish classes, proved popular in Britain. By May 1847 *Punch* was advocating total reliance on the government's new poor law and leaving Ireland to 'shift for herself for a year'.

Two developments were cited for hardening *Punch*'s (and by extension, British public opinion's) heart against Ireland. Both centred on the theme of Irish 'ingratitude'. Within two months of 'Union is strength', *Punch* had decided that the Irish were rejecting the proffered spade and relapsing into atavistic violence. In 'Height of impudence' (12 December 1846), John Bull is accosted by an Irishman begging alms to buy a 'blunderbuss'. In contrast to the earlier cartoon, the Irishman is no longer 'brother', but bears the simian features that were to become so familiar to *Punch*'s readers in later years. To some extent this shift reflected the views of the individual cartoonists; 'Union is strength' was drawn by Richard Doyle, a Catholic and of Irish descent (although as strongly anti-Repeal as his father, John Doyle of 'Political Sketches' fame). 'Height of impudence' was by John Leech, *Punch*'s regular cartoonist in these years, and a man whose *bete noires* featured 'Italian organ-grinders, Frenchmen and Hebrews' as well as the Irish. The anthropological theories of 'Celtic' degeneracy which informed such stereotypes of 'Paddy' were by no means

THE IRISH CINDERELLA AND HER HAUGHTY SISTERS,
BRITANNIA AND CALEDONIA.

18. The Irish Cinderella. (*Punch*)

universally accepted in 1840s Britain, but were mobilised forcefully for specific purposes in *Punch* and *The Times*. This transition period between the dominance of environmentalism and racialism as the leading discourse regarding Ireland was particularly disadvantageous to the country: while brute enough to require coercion, the Irish were seen as sufficiently 'normal' to be expected to exhibit self-reliance, and were denied the paternalistic relief later doled out by Dublin Castle in the subsistence crises of the 1880s and 1890s.

Punch came to support strict coercion of Ireland, the suppression of agrarian agitation, and the imprisonment of troublesome priests. Yet in line with its radical leanings, it expressed little sympathy for Irish landlords, who were depicted as ready to rob John Bull to line their own pockets and subsidise a lifestyle of cowardly absenteeism. The paper showed no sympathy for the developing campaign for tenant right, but – in the wake of *The Times* – moved towards advocating more drastic treatment of the Irish of all classes.

The second development that served to amplify such British antagonism was the growing political instability of Ireland. 'Union is strength' had suggested an optimistic outlook on Anglo–Irish relations, and *Punch* had gloated at Daniel O'Connell's apparent renunciation of repeal and request for greater British aid shortly before his death in 1847. In this context, the increasingly vociferous militancy of the nationalist Young Ireland movement provoked outrage and a further denunciation of the Irish as a whole. Leech went the full way with the simian stereotype by portraying the movement's most extreme leader, John Mitchel, as a monkey – at once comic and dangerously incendiary – threatening a magisterial and contemptuous British lion. ['The British lion and the Irish monkey', 8 April 1848] In the wake of the abortive 1848 rising, *Punch* returned repeatedly to the theme of inveterate Irish barbarity and ingratitude. Agrarian unrest and political rebellion were blended together, and images of famine-related suffering were ignored. British policy appeared incapable of ameliorating the situation through conciliation. In 'Alfred the small' (16 September 1848), the Prime Minister, Lord John Russell, is pictured visiting Ireland, only to find the primitive natives immersed in violence and idolatrously worshipping the totems of Repeal.

If *Punch*'s main political thrust lay in its chief cartoon – the subject of which was decided weekly by the principal contributors – the paper was always more than its 'big cut'. It carried numerous one-liners, squibs and articles on Irish subjects, as well as pieces of more sustained satire in verse and prose. W.M. Thackeray was the source of the bulk of its Irish pieces in these years. His *Irish Sketch Book* (1843), an impressionistic but largely critical account of an Irish visit, had proven a great success in England (not least for its strident anti-Catholicism). It was on the strength of this that he emerged as *Punch*'s Irish expert, often under the pseudonym 'Hibernis Hibernior'. In 'Mr *Punch* for Repeal' (26 February 1848) Thackeray declared that he had made a personal contribution of £5 to the British Association relief fund in early 1847, but as reasons for giving no more, went on to cite the support of certain Catholic clerics for the tenant movement (which Thackeray interpreted as a murderous conspiracy), and John O'Connell's criticism of the British state and press for failing to come to terms with the continuation of the famine. This clearly echoed the mood of British

THE REAL POTATO BLIGHT OF IRELAND.
(FROM A SKETCH TAKEN IN CONCILIATION HALL.)

19. The real potato blight. (*Punch*)

public opinion, for a second charitable appeal in October 1847 had proved an unpopular flop and no further substantial sums were raised. Thackeray also took up the cry for 'repeal' in an ironic sense, as a means of protecting England from further Irish mendicancy. These themes were reiterated in the 'Letters to a nobleman visiting Ireland' (2 and 9 September 1848), in which

UNION IS STRENGTH.

John Bull.—"HERE ARE A FEW THINGS TO GO ON WITH, BROTHER, AND I'LL SOON PUT YOU IN A WAY TO EARN YOUR OWN LIVING."

20. Union is strength. (*Punch*)

Lord John Russell was upbraided for his previous political connections with the O'Connells, and Irish poverty was attributed to Irish wrong-headedness.

Punch regularly criticised Russell for having no Irish policy, but also staunchly opposed government expenditure in Ireland. In the wake of the financial crisis of autumn 1847, British industry and commerce underwent a period of depression: middle-class radicals responded by crusading against taxation and landlord privileges. The general election of 1847 gave a group of about 85 radicals, led by Cobden, Bright and Hume, the parliamentary balance of power. Both Russell and Lord Lieutenant Clarendon were aware of the vital need for increased relief, development and emigration assistance spending to alleviate the crisis in Ireland, but they failed to make headway, being faced with ideological hostility from the advocates of 'natural causes' within the government and strenuous resistance from the commons. *Punch* expressed glee when Russell was forced to withdraw a proposed increase in the British income tax in his 1848 budget, and then outrage at every concession extracted to meet the extensive distress of the west of Ireland in 1848-49. Every loan to the ungrateful Irish, however small, was denounced as an additional burden on England's respectable poor. [The English Labourer's Burden', 24 February 1849]. It was indicative of just how deeply divided the Whig-Liberal cabinet was that such irresponsible press statements were welcomed and encouraged by some ministers. From late 1846 Charles Wood, Chancellor of the Exchequer, sought to undermine relief expenditure by stimulating a British backlash against the 'monstrous machine' of public works. He, Trevelyan and Colonial Secretary Lord Grey had close connections with Delane of *The Times* and exploited these for political ends. By autumn 1848, a broad swathe of British opinion was convinced that mass starvation was inevitable in Ireland, and should not be prevented. The diarist Charles Greville noted that the prevailing sense in London was 'disgust … at the state of Ireland and the incurable madness of the people'. The press had done much to create this perception. The Prime Minister was obliged to admit that it was less the 'crude Trevelyanism' of his subordinates than feelings lying 'deep in the breasts of the British people' that had made substantive intervention impossible.

As if exhausted or secretly embarrassed by its sustained hostility during a period of acute suffering and mass mortality, *Punch* sought for signs of hope in 1849. Two events were highlighted. The 'new plantation' scheme proposed by elder statesman Sir Robert Peel was warmly welcomed. Peel suggested a commission with sweeping powers over the west of Ireland that would pave the way for 'new proprietors who shall take possession of the land of Ireland, freed from its present encumbrances, and enter into its cultivation with adequate capital, with new feelings, and inspired by new hopes'. Richard Doyle pictured Peel as 'The new St Patrick', driving the reptiles of 'destitution', 'mortgages' (depicted by a Jewish stereotype) and 'famine' out of Ireland. Leech welcomed Peel's 'panacea' of 'the sale of encumbered estates' as the cure to Russell's 'dreadful Irish toothache'. The idea of a British economic 'colonisation', reclaiming the bogs of Connacht for civilisation, appealed strongly to the paper, and a mass removal of the 'biped livestock' by clearance and emigration was welcomed. ['A parallel between Peel and Caesar', 28 April 1849]. Yet, like *The Times*, its support was primarily for 'free trade in land' rather than full-scale government intervention. Peel had advocated relaxation of the poor law and increased state investment, but moralist opinion remained adamantly opposed.

The second event was the Queen's visit to Ireland in August 1849. The unifying mystique of the monarchy was sufficient for *Punch* to restore the image of a poor but welcoming 'Hibernia', and to transform the threatening 'Paddy' into the comically harmless 'Sir Patrick Raleigh'. ['Landing of Queen Victoria in Ireland', August 1849] *Punch* put its faith in the royal visit as the most efficacious mode of anglicising the country and its people, imagining an Ireland of the future built on the suppression of its past [Ireland – a dream of the Future, Sept. 1849]. This was wishful thinking, and the flood of private and corporate investment expected in the wake of the Queen's visit failed to materialise. Plans by the City of London corporation to purchase large tracts of Connacht also fell through.

Punch's vision of Irish prosperity arising simply from self-exertion – 'new' proprietors were primarily to provide entrepreneurial values rather than cash – proved illusory. Yet such was the depth of early Victorian liberal optimism that it refused to abandon the image of creating plenty through the application of industry to peat. ['The new Irish Still', August 1849] The idea would be ludicrous, were it not for the fact that this illusion, and the moralistic outrage directed against the Irish when it was not realised, underlay the response not only of *Punch*, but of the dominant strand of British public opinion, to the Great Famine. The specific political circumstances of the later 1840s entailed that this opinion played a considerable part in limiting the options available to a weak and deeply divided government. The present debate amongst historians over whether and where moral responsibility for the famine can be attributed would be illuminated if such aspects were sufficiently taken into account. Too detailed an analysis can perhaps detract from the wit and humour of nineteenth-century cartoons and comic writing. Yet these were not merely intended as amusing frivolities. They had real political significance and should be treated as historical documents. We should beware of too hastily passing judgement on the people of the past, but surely the performance of *Punch* can be evaluated in the light of its own critique of O'Connell in 1845:

'A joke is a joke, and nothing can be more pleasing … in its proper place – but not always. You wouldn't cut capers over a dead body, or be particularly boisterous and facetious in a chapel or a sick-room; and I think, of late … you have been allowing your humour to get the better of you on occasions almost as solemn. For, isn't hunger sacred? Isn't starvation solemn?'

When applied to Ireland, the answer appeared to be that it was not.

Chapter 4

The Irish Constabulary in the Great Famine

W.J. Lowe

In 1845 the Irish Constabulary, which was organized in its permanent form in 1836, was deployed countrywide to control agrarian crime. Even though fears of violence were high in provincial landlord and merchant circles during the Great Famine, the police mostly found themselves witnesses to human tragedy. The desperation of the famine produced some violent confrontations that involved the police, but, for all the tension, drama and seemingly interminable duty, policing the famine was mostly an extension of customary routines, which defined the Constabulary's post-famine role.

The constabulary became a familiar fixture in Ireland during the famine. The discipline and military bearing with which the police were associated were strictly maintained, as were the barrack routines laid down by the constabulary code. A constabulary function that was firmly institutionalised during the famine was collecting statistics. It may seem perversely mundane that Irishmen on the public payroll reduced the suffering of the famine years to numbers, but what the government and later generations know about the famine's impact owes a great deal to information recorded at the local level by the police and local magistrates.

The constabulary's role in districts seriously affected by hunger and disease derived almost entirely from its regular duties and assignments, but responsibilities were added as needs dictated. The pressure and duration of duty in famine-afflicted districts was unprecedented and would only be approached again during the Land War of the early 1880s and the Anglo-Irish War of 1919-21.

The Irish National Archives contain collections of papers that describe conditions in Ireland during the famine and the constabulary's activities. The Outrage Papers and the Chief Secretary's Office Registered Papers, for example, are organised by county for the famine period, which permits a detailed view of how the famine affected different areas, such as counties Clare, Galway, Mayo, and Tipperary. There are also collections of famine-era constabulary circulars held in the National Archives of the United Kingdom.

The constabulary's first assignment was to keep the misery of famine Ireland from erupting into violence that threatened property and property owners, and to maintain public order as defined at Dublin Castle and

Westminster. By January 1846 the Irish Government was receiving a steady stream of local reports that potatoes were scarce and the prices of provisions beyond the means of subsistence families. There were widespread fears about unrest and a Resident Magistrate (RM) wrote from Galway to ask that a warship and marines be sent to Galway Bay: 'The reports which I receive daily of the continued rot of the potatoes in the pits and in the houses are truly alarming. Potatoes are now from five pence to six pence per stone, wholesale…a famine price to the poor unemployed inhabitants…And I know not the moment an outbreak may take place'. He thought that a 'very large military force' was needed to preserve order because the twenty-eight resident Constabulary were wholly inadequate: 'The minds of the people are excited beyond measure. They are unemployed, they are without food…some evil is brooding'. Foreboding in the respectable public mind and reports of possible unrest were taken seriously. Within days cavalry, infantry and a steamer carrying marines arrived in Galway.

While crime related directly to destitution was a serious problem for the police during the famine, the large-scale rioting and plundering that so frightened provincial business and professional people did not occur. Still there were local problems and threats that steadily increased the demands on the police. Traditional agrarian crime declined as communities were affected by hunger, death and emigration. But there were large increases in offences of hunger and privation, such as burglary, robbery, livestock stealing, and plundering of provisions. Crime was at its highest levels in 1847, reported offences increasing by about 60 per cent over 1846. There were 10,000 reports of cattle and sheep stealing, 1,200 incidents of plundering of provisions and more than 1,000 reports of stealing weapons in 1847. Very few of these crimes resulted in arrests or convictions, but each required a police investigation.

The high incidence of petty, individual crimes prompted Edward Jones of Clonmel, Tipperary, to write that:

'The country is in a state of nearly perfect anarchy. Our police force is not sufficiently strong…From the way in which the people conduct themselves, they appear to believe that the restraining power of the law is removed. The well disposed and industrious feel uneasy for the safety of their property. They know and hear of cattle & sheep being killed and carried away; of boats & carts being plundered and of assaults & petty robberies being daily committed on almost every road.'

Large numbers of destitute families were compelled to leave their homes for failure to pay rent, to find subsistence or emigrate during the famine. So the roads were filled with people who appeared threatening and the Irish Constabulary, mostly deployed in four-and five-man stations, did not appear sufficiently imposing.

The government's public works programme also caused worry, given that it involved bringing large numbers of people together in a way that might facilitate organized disaffection. This sense that the scale of poverty could overwhelm local constabulary parties caused a great increase in requests for police during the famine. In 1847 alone, there were 131 requests for protection of individuals; 275 requests for increases in police (ranging from a few to 100 men); and 157 miscellaneous calls for extra police assistance.

Even the progressive increase in the size of the force during these years (from 9,100 in 1845 to 12,500 in 1850, with 1,265 extra constables recruited in 1846 alone) fell short of local expectations. Inhabitants of Louisburgh in Mayo petitioned for more police because they 'live in a wild, remote district and have reason to apprehend danger to their lives and properties, from the dreadful excitement that at present prevails by reason of the famine...[we] can expect but little defence against the infuriated populace from four police constables composing the whole force here'.

This is a good example of the type of pleas that reached Dublin Castle and the reception that most received. The cost of increasing a local police presence was shared between the Dublin Government and the local ratepayers. While additional protection was almost always seen as necessary, the accompanying cost to ratepayers was usually viewed as an outrage, threatening letters being almost preferable to notices of rate increases. Since few of the petitioners volunteered for higher rates, they were usually given a polite brush-off.

It is not surprising that some of the most common occasions of violence involved the transport of food and provisions to markets, warehouses, ports, or relief points. The resulting guard and escort duty so stretched police resources that a Galway RM wrote to Dublin Castle about the 'overworked police force...arising from the escorts they are obliged to furnish for the safe transit of provisions, their nightly patrols and escorting of pay clerks through the country'.

An elaborate system was needed so that available police and troops could handle different stages of provision carts' routes. Escorting was manpower and time intensive and Inspector General McGregor worried about the effects of prolonged heavy duty. When he was asked to increase off-road night patrols, he complained that 'they could but very imperfectly patrol their subdistrict were they even to march the whole night. But it must be remembered that these very men have also numerous indispensable duties to perform on the following day... The physical powers of even the Irish police...have their limits'.

Complaints, exaggerated reports and requests for augmented police presence comprised a great deal of the Constabulary-related paperwork generated by the famine. But the famine years figure as a time of extraordinarily heavy expenditure of police time and energy (they went almost everywhere on foot) in a variety of duties. The police sometimes had to confront the types of crime and disorder that the anxious memorials described, but most of the long hours spent by the Constabulary involved duties that varied from tediously routine to cruelly ironic.

The temporary government relief schemes of 1846 and 1847, public works projects and the soup kitchens that replaced them, required police supervision. The public works employed donkeys, whose owners were paid. An incident in Tipperary in January 1847 is an example of how easily tensions could escalate. A relief project required six donkeys and twelve animals were available. The local Board of Works steward, a Mr Cosgrave, hired six of the donkeys and then the other six, 'week and week about'. A donkey owner who wanted his donkey to work continuously brought an armed party to fire on Cosgrave's house.

By late 1846, there were robberies and attempted robberies of Board of Works clerks travelling to distribute wages at relief project sites. The Chief Secretary, Sir George Grey, recommended that pay clerks travel only with police escorts, but it was acknowledged that the 'numerous demands for escorts are more than the constabulary can furnish, as their stations usually consist of only five men, who have also to maintain a night patrol'. The police began to escort public works pay clerks and at least two policemen were shot dead in robberies.

There were also dangerous disputes over the rates of wages. At Lorrha, Tipperary, wages were reduced from 10d per day to 8d. An angry crowd of 400 left the road works to protest the wage reduction and drove seventy-two sheep from a field, 'to slaughter them for their own use'. The crowd and the sheep were pursued by Head Constable Rutledge and his six policemen, who reported that 'the language of the body of men was that of self-destitution [sic], such as they would suffer to be shot, that they might as well die there...that they would no longer suffer themselves to be in a state of starvation'. The head constable and the local Catholic curate subsequently persuaded the men to return the sheep to the field.

The transition from public works wages to soup kitchens was part of the government's effort to restrict famine relief and its cost to the local level. But the change stirred fears that government policy would result in disturbances because it was clear that people preferred even miserly public works employment to soup kitchens because they wished to retain some independence and control of their domestic lives. The Cashel magistrates drafted in additional police and cavalry and secured the co-operation of the Catholic clergy to keep things peaceful. At Littleton in Tipperary 'a large concourse of people' destroyed the boiler for the local relief committee's soup kitchen, 'there being no adequate police force successfully to resist so great a multitude'.

The constabulary's contact with the relief system involved much sadder duties. The most common evidence of the impact of hunger and disease was the finding of corpses. An example of the famine hardship that the police saw so regularly comes from Corofin, Clare, where Subconstable Michael Lynch investigated the death by starvation of John Coleman in May 1848. Coleman had a relief ticket for his family, but his wife was too ill to go to the workhouse; her 'body has the appearance of long fasting, and, by all accounts, they are a destitute family. I saw a bunch of withered nettles there which I was told to be intended for breakfast'. The coroner's verdict was that Coleman died 'for want of the common necessaries of life'.

The desperation of life in famine Ireland was manifested in other ways that directly involved the Constabulary. Bridget O'Dea was arrested for setting fire to a house near Scariff in order to be transported, since she had been refused relief. In that same neighborhood a man was shot dead for stealing potatoes by Edmond Stewart, who 'was exasperated at the time, as quantities of his potatoes had been frequently stolen before'.

The hardships of hunger and disease were compounded by clearances of thousands of small holdings for nonpayment of rent and to make way for the further expansion of grazing. Problems of collecting rents presented a convenient pretext to consolidate holdings. The Irish Constabulary did not actually take part in evictions, but frequently were on hand in case of trouble. The scale of famine-era clearances, as well as the density of population on small holdings, are starkly illustrated by a mass eviction on the property of John Gerrard, of Ballinlass, Galway, in March 1846. The Constabulary Sub-Inspector, Bernard Cummins, was called on to protect the sheriff's party with forty-five constables and ninety soldiers:

> 'Eighty houses were levelled to the ground and no resistance offered by the people, several of whom had cleared off previous to our going there. Eighty families consisting of upwards of 400 individuals were dispossessed. The townland contains about 500 acres.'
>
> 'The tenants and labourers of Mr Gerrard from another part of his property were obliged to attend there (very much against their will) in order to assist in levelling those houses.'

County Inspector W. Lewis added that 'the unfortunate people who were turned out are in a state of misery not to be described, scattered over this neighbourhood, living in the ditches, or anywhere they can find shelter to erect a hut in. Fortunately for them, they were allowed to take the timber of their cabins with them'.

Some clearances were resisted. A Mr Mannin of Dublin, who owned land in Tipperary, wrote to Dublin Castle to request assistance in clearing tenants and levelling their houses because his agent had been murdered in January 1847. Mannin's case was an opportunity for a clear explication of the constabulary's role in evictions and clearances: 'The police cannot be employed in pulling down houses or carrying out any other arrangements...but if an affidavit is made before a magistrate...that an outrage is likely to be committed upon those employed... in a lawful occupation, it is competent to such a magistrate to direct a patrol in the neighborhood'. Even at the height of the land agitation of the 1880s, the police protected but did not sanction evictions. Besides the potential danger to policemen actively participating in clearances of cottiers, there was also the matter of rank-and-file morale. Asking men who were the sons of tenant farmers to take an active part in evictions would have sorely tested the constabulary's discipline.

There were sufficient problems and excitement in the 1840s to keep the Irish Constabulary fully occupied with conditions directly related to the famine. But, foreshadowing the role they would occupy in the administration of Ireland for the next seventy-five years, there was yet another duty that absorbed a great deal of police attention and confronted hard-pressed farmers and the police in Ireland with the relentless banality of bureaucracy.

The government's progressive emphasis on making famine relief a local responsibility and expense meant that, even in the depths of the famine, tax collections were pursued aggressively. Even after the public works and soup kitchens were withdrawn, local relief costs could be very high and government at all levels was eager to capture as much tax revenue as possible. The establishment of the poor law system in Ireland in the late 1830s created a new local tax to be collected, the poor rate, and by the early 1840s resistance among tenant farmers to the payment of poor rates required a constabulary presence when bailiffs were sent to seize crops and livestock for non-payment.

During the famine even substantial tenants were affected by the fact that food was now more expensive, yet they were liable to heavier county and poor rates that left them sometimes unable and often disinclined to pay. From early 1847, as the famine's impact intensified, resistance to tax collection increased. Dublin Castle directed that poor rate and county cess (tax) collections should receive police protection, which quickly added to the pressure on police time and resources.

Even with a constabulary escort, collection sometimes failed. A bailiff protected by eight policemen seized cattle and sheep in Bansha, County Tipperary, and was then confronted by forty people blocking the road. The attempt to drive the livestock through the group resulted in the animals being recaptured. Those involved in the rescue were arrested, but resistance continued. By 1848, some collections were more successful and peaceful, but police and sometimes military protection was often on hand. Anywhere from twenty to fifty police might have to march from different stations.

The autumn of 1848 saw intense resistance to rate collections in County Clare. The rate collector for the Gort union went to Cranagh without his police and military escorts. His twenty carts were damaged and harnesses cut by stone-throwing men and women. When the police arrived, the crowd was barricading the road, but the police declined to act without the authorisation of the RM. A couple of carts approached the grain intended for seizure, but they were damaged, the drivers injured and nothing seized. Several stonethrowers were arrested, but freed, so that the police would not be burdened with prisoners in a dangerous situation.

News of what happened at Cranagh spread quickly in north Clare and threats and resistance continued. The situation was complicated by the fact that two important sectors of the rural establishment were competing with each other for tenant farmers' scant resources. The landlords were owed the entire crop intended for taxes and they were trying to cart it off ahead of the rate collectors. The collector at Milrook, one Mr Glynn, was advised that 'the next time you come, bring your coffin, for you'll require it'. Glynn concluded that 'the people of that village are unquestionably very poor, and have scarcely any means, but whatever corn they had, which is seized by the landlord'. At Arran, the bailiff was confronted by angry women, who refused to let him pass. They warned him that:

'No matter what number of police I brought with me, they would treat them and my men in the same way as they were treated in Grennagh [sic] the day before...It is perfectly impossible for me to bring a single beast or a grain of corn out of it without a strong force. This village certainly is very poor, as they live on the seaside and depended hitherto on the seaweed and potato. The potato is now gone and, consequently, there is no demand for the seaweed [as fertilizer].'

An expedition of 100 police and troops failed at Kinvara and of the Cranagh incident 'it is generally reported throughout the union that the police and military were defeated'. The resistance that Cranagh inspired created the opening through which:

'The stock of corn, in numerous cases the only stake for the rate, is rapidly disappearing from the lands of many of the farmers...In a very short period there will be nothing left on these premises available for payment, and the occupiers, by their violent and lawless proceedings, will secure exemption from this rate as well as from the last.'

The people so described by the Gort board of guardians were not poor relief recipients but tenant farmers who had crops to sell and rents to pay, which shows the long social and economic reach of the famine crisis and the ways in which government relief policies affected communities. Rate collection, like evictions and provision escorts, caused very long days for the Irish Constabulary, who often marched long distances in the face of popular disapproval, if not open opposition.

Policing famine Ireland involved extended hours of duty, the threat of violence and the enforcement of the law in the face of human suffering. The police were constantly in the presence of the poor and destitute, presiding at relief programs or evictions and escorting provisions and rate collectors. There were severe emotional, morale and physical costs to such prolonged stress of duty and exposure to epidemic disease: the three years 1847, 1848 and 1849 accounted for the highest-ever active-duty death rates, about twice as high as the average for the entire period 1841-1914. The incidence of gratuities to policemen who left the force prior to being pensionable also rose to their highest level in 1847.

The rate of resignation also began to accelerate during the famine. Inspector General McGregor worried in 1848 that 'many of our respectable men have sought refuge from such excessive work by withdrawing altogether from the force...young men of character having begun within the last twelve or eighteen months to refuse entering constabulary service notwithstanding the general want of employment'. The intense activity during the famine accelerated the consolidation of constabulary roles and duties that continued until disbandment in 1922 and the police were established as a permanent local presence. But Irish policemen did not escape the toll exacted by the famine.

Chapter 5

The Great Famine general election of 1847

Brian Walker

The ultimate responsibility for the failure to cope effectively with the disaster of the Great Famine lay with the Westminster parliament, but we should remember that Ireland in 1847 returned 105 MPs to Westminster. A unified effort by all these MPs could have changed government policies. No such agreed approach emerged and there was a serious failure among Irish politicians and electors to respond to the ongoing crisis in a meaningful way.

The context of the ongoing famine in August 1847 must be appreciated. The famine had begun in the second half of 1845. Failure of the potato crop that year and in 1846 led to massive loss of life and forced emigration. By the summer of 1847, however, it seemed that the worst was over. In July and August of that year the Irish press carried many glowing reports of good harvests. Unfortunately, the crops planted were small in quantity, and severe suffering would ensue in late 1847 and into 1848. The blight would return in 1848 and 1849, with terrible consequences.

Different measures, public and private, were taken during these five years to combat the famine, but many of these proved very inadequate. Nonetheless, the government-run food and soup kitchens and depots, which were established in early 1847, enjoyed considerable success. This scheme was wound up in August 1847, partly because it was believed that the bad times were over and partly because the government, in its attachment to laissez-faire policies, introduced a new relief scheme, which meant that famine relief would be handled locally by Poor Law unions.

The renewed crisis from late 1847, however, showed how inadequate was this policy of relying on local resources to cope with the famine. Poor Law Unions in the worst-affected areas were overwhelmed by the numbers involved, and there was a failure to adequately back up local efforts by assistance from central funds. The next two years would witness serious loss of life and massive emigration.

Elections in this period were not the democratic events we know today. There was a very restrictive property franchise. Less than two per cent of the population had the vote. Women were excluded entirely. Nonetheless, candidates usually held public meetings attended by large numbers of people. Political issues were enthusiastically discussed on these occasions and there was a very active press.

The majority of Irish politicians were Protestant and landowners. Since Catholic emancipation, however, there were significant numbers of Catholics and professional people among the politicians. The main parties, simply put, were the Conservatives (Tories) who sought to protect the existing constitutional position, the Liberals (Whigs) who wanted moderate reforms, the repealers who advocated repeal of the union as advocated by Daniel O'Connell, and the confederates who took a more radical position.

Political priorities during the 1847 general election are revealed in the candidates' printed addresses and nomination speeches, which were recorded in local newspapers. From the evidence of this material, it is clear that the famine was not the dominant subject of discussion during August 1847. Many seem to have believed that the worst was over and were unaware that they were in the middle of a national catastrophe. The main public concerns of most politicians continued to revolve around questions of the 'constitution', 'repeal' or 'civil and religious liberty'. In spite of talk earlier in 1847 of Irish politicians coming

21. *An Irish Eviction* (1850) by Frederick Goodall. During the Famine mass evictions led to forced emigration. (Leicester Museum & Art Gallery)

together to deal with the famine, this did not happen and politicians fought the elections over the usual issues.

In some places the famine received very little mention. For example, in Galway town, where two repeal candidates, M. J. Blake and Anthony O'Flaherty, were returned unopposed, the famine was almost entirely ignored in their addresses and nomination speeches. Shortly after the election a large public repeal dinner was held to celebrate the election outcome. One of the candidates refused to attend, on the grounds that 'during this season of famine and pestilence, a festivity of this sort is at least unseemly'. Nonetheless, the dinner went ahead. The *Galway Vindicator* declared: 'The patriots of Galway of every class participated in it, from the clergy and merchants to the honest and independent trades'.

In other constituencies, however, more attention was paid to the famine. Rarely was it the main subject, but politicians did express grave concern about the 'awful and critical times', the 'many sorrows and lamentations' and 'the deep abyss of our country's calamities and wrongs'. In County Mayo, the successful liberal candidate, George Moore, described how 'the evils that have resulted from the last fatal year have been numerous and dark and deadly' and he criticised current

22. Alexis Soyer's model soup kitchen in Dublin. Government-run soup kitchens, which had proved relatively successful, were wound down in August 1847, partly because it was believed that the worst was over. (*Illustrated London News*)

23. An attack on a potato store by starving people. At no stage was the idea of banning food exports a subject for debate during the general election. (*Illustrated London News*)

relief measures, while the successful repeal candidate, R. D. Browne, declared his aim 'to combine all parties for the common good of the country'. Politicians often put forward proposals to improve conditions in Ireland, but these were usually long- rather than short-term measures, such as land law reform.

Some omissions must be remarked upon. One of the most glaring was lack of criticism of the Gregory clause, which was part of the new relief measures passed earlier in the year and which would later have damaging consequences because it aimed to limit aid to those who occupied land of a quarter-acre or under. There was virtually no reference to this matter during the general election. In Dublin city, where Sir William Gregory, the author of the clause, was one of the outgoing Conservative MPs, he was challenged by a repealer over the clause, but mainly on the grounds that it 'must have the effect of swamping Dublin and the other large towns in Ireland by the paupers from their rural districts', rather than from concern about its effects on smallholders.

A number of candidates deplored conditions aboard emigrant ships, but none appear to have advocated specific reforms of the navigation laws. No support or appreciation was expressed for an address from the Canadian parliament calling

24. Typical scene at an Irish 'open house' after the poll. Meetings before (and after) elections were opportunities for many people, electors and non-electors alike, to engage in political debate and robust entertainment. (*Illustrated London News*)

for various improvements in shipping conditions, and no criticism was voiced over a new passenger act, which had become law in July 1847 and which would require significant amendments in subsequent years.

In mid-August the main method of famine relief changed from government-run food kitchens and depots (which had proved successful) to reliance on Poor Law unions (which would prove unsuccessful), but there was remarkably little discussion of these significant changes. Virtually no one questioned the closing of the emergency food depots. Most concern expressed for those on the land was for farmers, and very seldom was there comment on the plight of the landless labourers or small cottiers. At no stage was the idea of banning food exports a subject for debate during the general election.

Ironically, many repealers were more restrained than Conservatives in their criticism of the government, because in a range of policies they preferred a Liberal Government to a Conservative one. The result of the general election was thirty-four repealers, two confederates, twenty-nine Liberals and forty Conservatives, an increase in the number of repealers at the expense of Liberals. In Great Britain the Liberals won just 269 out of 551 seats which meant they could only form a minority government. This outcome should have given great power at Westminster to the 105 Irish MPs, especially the repealers, now led by John O'Connell, after his father's death.

At other times, Irish parties have used their influence with minority British governments to advantage, as seen with the Irish Parliamentary Party in 1885-86 and the Democratic Unionist Party at present. In another effective tactic, Sinn Féin in 1918 declined to take their seats at Westminster. On this occasion, however, Irish MPs failed to take advantage of the situation and over the next five years they exercised little or no influence on Government policies for Ireland. A majority of Irish MPs, Liberals and repealers, returned to Westminster to support a minority Liberal Government.

Some explanations can be offered for why the subject of the famine did not receive greater and more constructive attention during the August 1847 general election. We can observe some of these factors in our own failures to effectively tackle modern-day famines and problems. Clearly, there was what may be called an 'information deficit' about what had happened and was continuing to happen. People spoke of an 'awful famine' but the figures of the number of people who had died ranged very widely, from several hundreds of thousands to two million. It was widely believed that the worst was over, which was a case of wishful thinking for many. Some candidates referred to the good harvests and talked about the 'past famine', although others did refer to the ongoing crisis. It is incredible that only a few individuals gave warning of the small quantities of potato crops planted. Their words of concern, however, were simply disregarded by the vast majority of politicians and electors, and it was not until late August and early September that public opinion began to wake up to this problem.

In famine situations today we often see the difficulties created by inadequate information. Now, as then, unreliable or false figures make it difficult to tackle these matters. At the same time, however, people are often unable or unwilling to take the real picture on board and they hope that matters will somehow sort themselves out. It can be recalled how in Ireland in recent years most people refused to recognise the inherent dangers of the housing boom.

In addition, ideological and party constraints hampered effective handling of these problems and prevented people from confronting the reality of the situation. The main concerns of most politicians continued to revolve around 'traditional' matters such as the 'union' or 'repeal'. In the political context of the time, these matters seemed to be of primary importance. Because of ideological constraints, people were not able to come up with new ideas or alliances to tackle the crisis, or to think outside the box.

We have seen how in the Ireland of the 1950s people failed to tackle the real problems, such as massive emigration in the South and a divided society in the North, because they believed that other issues, such as partition, were more important. Recent decades, however, have shown how politicians, in both Northern Ireland and the Republic of Ireland, could take new approaches that achieved considerable success.

There was widespread debate during the 1847 general election, but little of this involved the cottiers and labourers who were the worst affected by the famine and who were not part of the political system. They were the weakest members of society and the political classes were insufficiently concerned about their plight. One does not need to look far in the modern world to observe similar failings in political systems.

Other explanations can be offered, such as the 'law of unintended consequences', as seen in the Gregory clause, which its originator introduced to prevent the abuse of famine relief by better-off farmers but which proved harmful for many. Not just Gregory but very few others in Ireland in August 1847 realised the future detrimental effects of this clause. There are plentiful examples today of measures that bring results that were not intended.

In conclusion, it seems fair to state that Irish politicians and electors in mid-1847 could have responded more constructively to the Great Famine. With the benefit of hindsight, we know that after August 1847 matters would deteriorate again very seriously. An effective system to deal with this ongoing situation had not been put in place. Various immediate measures should have been supported, such as the continuation of emergency food depots or improvements in shipping conditions.

Owing to ideological and party constraints, Irish politicians were unable to operate outside existing alliances or ways of thinking. The chance was lost to bring a single, multi-party approach of 105 Irish MPs to the problem of the famine and to pressurise the government over its mishandling of the situation. In the light of these possibilities and failings, it is reasonable to argue that the general election of 1847 represented a missed opportunity for the political classes of Ireland to take steps to avert some of the worst effects of the Great Famine.

Chapter 6

The triumph of dogma: Ideology and famine relief

Peter Gray

How far can British Government be held responsible for the famine mortality of over one million in five years? What were the ideological motivations and constraints on ministers, and the effects of these on the formation of policy, particularly in the worst years of the famine from mid-1846 to mid-1849? By ideology is meant the framework of ideas—the world-view—that shaped how individuals and groups perceived the problems that faced them. Ideological constructions shaped the interpretation of catastrophes like the potato blight. They were significant in determining what were acceptable modes and levels of response to the crisis, giving legitimacy to some and not to others. Ideology must also be considered in a dynamic sense as the competition of rival ideas for political supremacy. So if the role of ideology is to be properly understood, it must be linked to a detailed study of the political history of the famine years, and of the broader public and intellectual context of British politics.

The allocation of responsibility for actions a century and half ago poses serious problems. Historians risk falling into gross anachronism in attempting to pass judgement on long-dead individuals. Yet the attempt should be made. The question then arises whether intentions or consequences should be the criteria for judgement. Any neglect of the adverse consequences of policy may be treated as culpable, if it can be shown that these were public knowledge. Yet it is the active intentions of policy-makers that may be considered more reprehensible. An evaluation of responsibility thus requires an understanding of the debates of the time, and the existence of feasible alternative policies. That such choices were perceived to exist, and that they were linked to ideological differences, is suggested by Lord Clarendon's agitated appeal to the Prime Minister in August 1847: 'We shall be equally blamed for keeping [the Irish] alive or letting them die and we have only to select between the censure of the economists or the philanthropists—which do you prefer?'

Before considering some of the crucial decisions taken by the government, the main ideological and political groupings need to be sketched out. The tradition which has often attracted most attention is that of classical political economy. The leading practitioners of this increasingly technical 'orthodox' system were anxious by the 1840s not only to refine economic theory, but to translate it into policy. They included Nassau Senior, G.C. Lewis, and Richard Whately. Politically, they were associated with the 'Bowood set' presided over by the Whig Lord Lansdowne, which included Lord Monteagle and other moderate liberals. Orthodox economists were, however, partisans more of policy than of party, and often looked as much to liberal Conservatives such as Sir Robert Peel. Malthus and Ricardo had been pessimistic about Irish over-population and underdevelopment, but the next generation of economists were generally more hopeful about the growth of agricultural productivity at a rate faster than that of population. Encouraging capital investment in land became their priority, along with guaranteeing security for freedom of outlay and certainty of return. To be successful, a re-organisation of landholding was declared essential, as they held that only large-scale capitalist farming on the English model could be efficient. Greater productivity would provide increased and more regular employment for labour; higher expectations and consumption would be made possible by the replacement of subsistence crops by wages.

Senior and his associates resolutely opposed the extension of a compulsory poor law to Ireland, on the grounds that, in such a poor country, it would drain scarce resources away from employment into 'useless' relief to the able-bodied. Yet the failure to prevent Whig governments introducing a limited Irish poor

A SCENE IN CAHIRCIVEEN. — A WIDOW AND CHILDREN OF THE O'CONNELL ESTATES ON THEIR WAY TO BEG POTATOES.

25. Irish poverty increasingly preoccupied British observers. This sketch from O'Connell's Co.Kerry estate appeared in early 1846. (*Illustrated London News*)

law in 1838, and then extending this as the central plank of famine-relief policy in 1847, demonstrates the limited influence of Senior over policy-making at pivotal times. Orthodox economics was more important in the broad appeal of its arguments for rejecting experiments with existing property rights, and for producing a climate of opinion that prioritised economic development over the relief of suffering, even in conditions of social catastrophe.

Several variant forms of economic thought were at least as significant. What became known as the 'Manchester school' was more radical, extreme and optimistic. It drew on general principles of orthodox thought, such as the desirability of free trade and laissez-faire, popularised them and made them more dogmatic. Lacking any outstanding theorists, this group was committed to campaigning for changes in policy, and was most influential among the politicised middle classes and in the liberal press. The Anti-Corn Law League was its initial focus; after 1846 it turned towards a more direct assault on landowners and their social privileges as obstacles to economic development. This class antagonism differentiated the Manchester school from orthodox thinkers, but more important was their adherence to a labour theory of value—the doctrine that capital is merely accumulated labour. From this flowed the idea that economic backwardness stemmed not from under-capitalisation, but from restrictions on the freedom of labour and the use of resources. When applied to Ireland these

26. New Government. Many hoped the new Whig Government formed in July 1846 would bring 'Justice to Ireland'. They were rapidly disillusioned. (*Illustrated London News*)

ideas rejected Malthusian pessimism entirely: Ireland was seen as a potentially wealthy country that could support several times its current population. What was required were measures to force Irish landowners to employ the poor, and a 'free trade in land' to replace them with agricultural entrepreneurs if the current owners failed.

A second offshoot from classical economics was that associated with a smaller group of heterodox writers. Theoretically more sophisticated than the

YANKEE DOODLE'S CORN EXCHANGE.

27. Yankee Doodle's Corn Exchange. This American cartoon praises that country's ability to feed Ireland from it's surplus grain;but it is unclear just how the desitute were expected to purchase such supplies. (*Yankee Doodle*)

Manchester school, they shared much of its optimism and criticism of aristocracy. They differed most in their support for alternative models of Irish development to that of crude anglicisation. William Thornton, J.S. Mill and Poulett Scrope agreed that it was the relationship of landlord and tenant that lay at the root of Irish economic backwardness: all looked positively on the alternative model of peasant proprietorship existing in other European countries. Once predatory landlordism had been restrained and peasants secured in their holdings, they believed the possession of property in itself would create the necessary motivation for investment and exertion from below. Detailed suggestions as to how such a revolution in agrarian power-relationships could be brought about were more troublesome, but all these writers agreed that the famine presented the government with an opportunity to intervene to reconstruct Irish society, preferably by confiscating waste and uncultivated lands for reclamation by the rural poor.

For a number of Whig politicians anxious to defuse the cry for repeal by granting a measure of 'Justice to Ireland', such ideas were particularly attractive. Lord John Russell and his Lord Lieutenant Lord Bessborough had a reputation for reformist co-operation with O'Connell. They identified themselves with the populist or 'Foxite' tradition of Whiggery rather than with orthodox liberalism, and were anxious to introduce more ambitious schemes for Ireland in 1846. The intensification of the famine was to expose both the limitations of this commitment and their political weakness, but the interventionist leanings of this group should not be underestimated.

All these schools of thought interpreted the famine disaster in the light of their own diagnoses of the 'Irish problem' and plans for Irish reconstruction. The very scale of the crisis tended to push each towards an inflexible insistence on their own panaceas. These economic ideologies were in turn variously affected by a pervasive religious mode of thought—providentialism, the doctrine that human affairs are regulated by divine agency for human good. More an interpretative language than a unified body of thought, providentialism took several forms. What concerns us here is the extent to which ideological stances on the famine were validated and intensified by the widespread belief that the potato blight had been sent by God for an ascertainable purpose.

Evangelical (or 'ultra') Protestants predictably saw the blight as divine vengeance against Irish Catholicism and on the British state that had recently committed such national 'sins' as endowing the Catholic seminary at Maynooth. Many more interpreted the 'visitation' of famine as a warning against personal and national pride and extravagance, and as an inducement to engage in charitable works. The Christian duty of charity continued to dominate the actions of groups like the Quakers, but for many in Britain, philanthropic feelings existed alongside a strong desire to see the fundamental changes in Ireland

A MARVELLOUS CURE.

Nurse Clarendon—" ALL OF A SUDDEN, SIR, HE BROKE OUT, RASH LIKE, ALL OVER, AND WENT ON IN A SHOCKING MANNER—IT WAS QUITE AWFUL TO HEAR HIM.   HE SAID HE 'D MURDER ME, AND YOU, AND I DON'T KNOW WHO ELSE; BUT HE 'S BEEN MUCH BETTER SINCE I PUT ON THE STRAIT-JACKET, AS YOU TOLD ME."

Doctor Russell—" AH! I KNEW THAT WOULD QUIET HIM."

28. A Marvellous Cure. Russell and Clarendon discuss how to cure 'Paddy', who is under the sedation of the coercion acts. (*Puppet Show*)

they believed would prevent the need for continuous private generosity. What gave providentialism some degree of ideological coherence was the existence of a Christian political economy that had evolved alongside the classical tradition in economics. Clerical economists had a profound influence over a British social elite that was imbued with the ethos of evangelical Protestantism. They urged governments to remove restrictions to economic freedom less to promote economic growth, than to subject individuals to the moral discipline of the 'natural' economic laws instituted by God. Acts of providence, such as the potato blight, could be interpreted in this tradition as a boon. Sir Robert Peel's linking of the potato blight of 1845 to the policy of removing the corn laws can be read in this light. The British obsession with free trade in food from 1846 reflected the power of this ideological connection.

Many of the Christian political economists were conservative, and had most influence over Peel and his followers. Popularised and radicalised forms of the doctrine had a greater impact on the early-Victorian middle classes and their political leaders. Providentialism blended with Manchester-school economics to produce a moralistic reading of the Irish crisis that put the blame for the state of society squarely on the moral failings of Irishmen of all classes. Consequently, the famine was welcomed as a God-given opportunity to enforce a policy that would transform Irish behaviour. Moralism was embraced by Whigs such as Earl Grey, Charles Wood, George Grey and the civil servant Charles Trevelyan, who sought to place themselves at the head of radical public opinion, and who were deeply infused with evangelical piety. To Trevelyan the blight was 'the cure...applied by the direct stroke of an all wise providence in a manner as unexpected and unthought of as it is likely to be effectual'.

Government officials in Ireland were no more immune to the prevailing moods of opinion than were ministers. Nevertheless, administrators on the ground in Ireland were developing an ethos of their own, that to some extent counter-balanced orthodox or moralist obsessions with the economy as a whole. A Benthamite concern for the efficient operations of institutions established for specified purposes—to distribute food, to organise public works and to provide relief through the poor law—stressed the immediate and the welfare aspects of state action rather than the long-term consequences. The impact of this administrative ideology was curbed by Trevelyan's dictatorial omniscience at the Treasury and frustrated both by a lack of resources and local resistance, but it became the dominant attitude of a Dublin executive increasingly at odds with London.

The second and total potato failure fell on a Whig-Liberal minority Government led by Lord John Russell that was more a coalition of 'reformers' than a unified party with a shared ideological position, and was subject to shifting political balances in parliament and in the country. Irish policy was a point of contention for the various party factions. Virtually the government's only shared commitment was to upholding free trade against any revived protectionist threat. This conspired to rule out anything more than marginal tinkering with the Irish food supply, with fateful consequences in the terrible winter of 1846-47.

By 1846 it was widely believed in British political circles that Ireland could never return to its previous condition, and that a great and inevitable social

PEEL'S PANACEA FOR IRELAND.

Russell. " OH ! THIS DREADFUL IRISH TOOTHACHE ! "
Peel. " WELL, HERE IS SOMETHING THAT WILL CURE YOU IN AN INSTANT."

29. Irish panacea. Peel presents Russell with a panacea for the 'dreadful Irish toothache'—the encumbered estates bill. (*Punch*)

revolution was under way. Interpretations varied according to attitudes towards Irish landlordism and widely divergent beliefs about the size of the Irish wages-fund: that is, the amount of capital that could be mobilised to employ labour. Irish landlords claimed that this was at an absolute minimal level, and demanded state help to promote development. English Conservatives and moderate

Liberals usually agreed that the wages-fund was low and that long-term aid through works projects and drainage loans was desirable, while remaining critical of the lax attitudes of many landlords. Russell's circle was not averse to state investment in the Irish infrastructure, but they shared a tendency with moralists and radicals to see the wages-fund as high, believing that landlords and large farmers were squandering or hoarding their resources, which they had amassed by ruthlessly exploiting the peasantry. Moralists parted company with others in claiming that the destitute population could be supported and the economy reconstructed simultaneously by measures of economic coercion. It was not enough for relief measures to provide the poor with the means of survival; they should do so in such a way as to discourage a culture of dependency and coerce the proprietors into undertaking their moral responsibilities.

The moralists sought to control Irish policy from 1846, but did not have it all their own way. Adjustments made to the public works legislation inherited from Peel were limited and were intended to eliminate abuse and manipulation by landlords and farmers. By December 1846, however, reports of the horrors of mass starvation at Skibbereen and other places demonstrated that traditional forms of relief were failing.

The initiative behind the radical departures agreed in January 1847 came primarily from the professional administrators of the Board of Works, who argued that labour and relief should be kept conceptually and practically apart. Public works relief had produced little of value at vast expense, had drained labour from agricultural cultivation, and had failed to save the masses of the poor from death. Bessborough and Russell conceded that the scale of the 1846-47 crisis demanded humanitarian aid in food, followed by the permanent extension of the poor law to give a right to relief to the able-bodied. The principle of relief by the poor law attracted consensus in January 1847 because it meant different things to different people and because the existing system was clearly indefensible. It was only on its implementation that the huge gulf of interpretative differences became manifest.

The soup kitchens act of February 1847 was an unprecedented innovation, but a temporary and transitional one. The political circumstances that allowed the act to pass also constrained it to a fixed period of time. British public opinion, stirred by a genuine, if ill-informed and temperamental humanitarianism, was prepared to accept a degree of state intervention until the harvest (so long as Irish ratepayers would ultimately be liable). The feeling remained strong that responsibility lay with the proprietors who had exploited the rise of a potato-dependent 'surplus' population, and that they should be made to pay for the costs of social transition. This was the logic, shared by most parliamentary liberals, that lay behind the decision to throw relief on the poor law as soon as what was widely seen as an exceptional season ended. What was at issue in the parliamentary session of 1847 was whether any concessions should be made to landlords in the working of the act, and what degree of government help for economic reconstruction should be provided.

Russell's waste land reclamation bill, drawn up in co-operation with his Foxite colleagues, was central to his legislative plan in 1847. The scheme was a radical one—to create peasant proprietors on Irish waste lands reclaimed with state aid. This bill was similar to schemes advocated by Mill and by Scrope. However, the measure was trimmed in cabinet by moderates anxious for the security of property rights, and then savaged in parliament by Peel and Stanley as an unwarranted interference with private enterprise, and Russell was forced to drop it. No major remedial scheme took its place.

The 1847 poor law bill was rejected in principle by orthodox thinkers; Senior had become convinced by this time that the potato failure had left Ireland over-populated by a redundant mass of two million people, and that there were no safe means of giving outdoor relief. His position was, however, compromised by the intransigent opposition of Irish landlords led by Monteagle and Whately, which did nothing but confirm parliament's insistence on the bill. The character of the measure was, however, substantially altered by amendments forced by Stanley as the English Conservatives' price for allowing it through the Lords. Chief amongst these was William Gregory's quarter acre clause, which denied relief to tenants holding more than a quarter of an acre of land, and which turned the act into a charter for clearance and consolidation. A cabinet majority of moderates and moralists supported the Gregory clause as a weapon necessary for forcing the pace of transition to an anglicised social and economic structure.

The British Government deserves most criticism for abandoning Ireland with only the poor law for support from autumn 1847. Vast American imports made food readily available and the state had proved its administrative capacity by providing up to three million daily rations in summer 1847 at an unexpectedly low cost, yet little was done to meet the widespread destitution that continued to summer 1849 and beyond. For at least part of the explanation we must look to the strengthening of the moralists' hand in summer 1847. A general election produced a small majority of Whig-Liberal MPs, many of whom were middle-class radicals who looked to Cobden, Bright and Hume for leadership. After several ministerial defeats, Russell drew the conclusion that 'we have in the opinion of Great Britain done too much for Ireland and have lost elections for doing so'. As the radicals came to hold the balance of power, Wood and Grey were further empowered. Secondly, the potato did not fail in 1847; few were planted and few harvested, but the apparent absence of any direct sign of divine intent allowed Trevelyan to declare that the famine was over, and that no further extraordinary measures could be justified.

Popular feelings on this were reinforced by the British banking crisis and financial crash of October 1847, which further boosted radicalism in its obsessive drive to retrench state expenditure. Government relief in Ireland was particularly targeted. Wood was thus not overly dismayed by the defeat of the 1848 budget, which had included a substantial increase in British income tax to meet the weight of Irish and defence expenditure, and which had been introduced by Russell. The setback allowed him to use the excuse that 'the British people have made up their minds to pay no more for Irish landlords' to reject Clarendon's increasingly frantic appeals for more aid. Russell's attempts to circumvent this obstacle by means of a state loan were blocked in cabinet by an alliance of moralists threatening a revolt of 'distressed English manufacturers' and moderates rejecting any additional taxation on Irish land or incomes.

There is no doubt that traditional anti-Irishness played a role in this British hostility; racial and cultural stereotypes were common in the press. An upsurge of agrarian violence in late 1847, and the nationalist activity culminating in the abortive rebellion of 1848, further convinced many of Irish ingratitude for English 'generosity' in 1847. Yet the most striking aspect of British opinion was the inclusion of Irish landowners in this moral censure. When the potato failed again in 1848, the dominant view was that Providence had again intervened to discipline all classes into the exertion and self-reliance necessary to maximise the use of undeveloped Irish resources.

Within a few months of his arrival in July 1847, the new Lord Lieutenant Clarendon had come under the influence of the senior Irish administrators, and shared their view that the saving of human life was imperative. While continuing to defend the broad outlines of government policy when pressed by Irish landlords, he demanded increased grants to assist the impoverished areas where the poor law was collapsing, and to introduce assisted emigration and other remedial measures. Clarendon and Russell collaborated in drawing up remedial proposals, but all these proved abortive. Russell had lost authority over his cabinet, and found his own position increasingly marked by confusion and indecision in the face of ideological certainty. On the failure of anything but the most modest of measures, he fell back on self-justifying rhetorical defences based on his continuing antagonism towards landlords, and on the supposed inevitability of mass suffering. Unable to choose between the imperatives of philanthropy and economy, Russell sought to steer an untenable middle course, and in the process presided over the decimation of the Irish people.

While British opinion rejected further spending in Ireland, it also demanded more constructive reforms. In 1849 parliament swung behind Peel's suggestion of a strong measure to force the sale of encumbered estates to new, active proprietors. Moralists like Wood had long been committed to an encumbered estates bill as the best mode of facilitating social transition in the west by sweeping away the existing irresponsible or indebted owners and replacing them with men of different values and available capital. To Wood, as to Peel, free trade in land was the logical climax of response to the Irish crisis that had made free trade in corn so vital in 1845-46.

In retrospect, the most realistic alternative to the moralist relief policy was presented by the Irish executive and administration under Bessborough and Clarendon. Although bound by the constraints of early Victorian administrative thinking, the Irish administration was probably the most advanced and interventionist in Europe. Its senior officers recognised that the crisis of relief resolved ultimately into distributing money to specific areas and needs. Their bitterness at the state's unwillingness or inability to respond effectively to the crisis is demonstrated by Twistleton's decision to resign over the termination of all direct parliamentary subsidies and the planned imposition of the rate-in-aid in spring 1849. Clarendon explained Twistleton's motives: 'He thinks the destitution here is so horrible, the indifference of the House of Commons to it so manifest, that he is an unfit agent of a policy that must be one of extermination'.

The policy pursued from autumn 1847, against the advice of expert administrators, can only be condemned as adding profusely to Ireland's misery. It is difficult to refute the indictment made by one humanitarian English observer in the later stages of the famine, that amidst 'an abundance of cheap food...very many have been done to death by pure tyranny'. The charge of culpable neglect of the consequences of policies leading to mass starvation is indisputable. That a conscious choice to pursue moral or economic objectives at the expense of human life was made by several ministers can also be demonstrated. Russell's government can thus be held responsible for a failure to honour its own 1846 pledge to use 'the whole credit of the Treasury and the means of the country...as is our bounden duty to use them...to avert famine, and to maintain the people of Ireland'.

Yet to single out the government alone for blame is to oversimplify. What ruled out alternative policies was the strength of the British public opinion manifested in parliament. During the famine years the British economy went through a crisis that mobilised an assertive middle-class political opinion. Amid the confusion, those most in line with this sentiment, and those (as in the cases of Wood and Trevelyan) ready to exploit it, were at a political advantage. Thus the ideas of moralism, supported by Providentialism and a Manchester-school reading of classical economics, proved the most potent of British interpretations of the Irish famine. What these led to was not a policy of deliberate genocide, but a dogmatic refusal to recognise that measures intended 'to encourage industry, to do battle with sloth and despair; to awake a manly feeling of inward confidence and reliance on the justice of heaven' (in the words of Anthony Trollope), were based on false premises, and in the Irish conditions of the later 1840s amounted to a sentence of death on hundreds of thousands of people.

Chapter 7

Food exports from Ireland, 1846-47

Christine Kinealy

'Let us explain to you Irish farmer, Irish landlord, Irish labourer, Irish tradesman, what became of your harvest, which is your only wealth. Early in the   winter it was conveyed, by the 1000 shiploads, to England, paying freight; it was stored in   English stores, paying storage; it was passed from hand to hand among corn-speculators, paying at every remove, commission, merchants' profits, forwarding charges and so forth: some of it was bought by French or Belgian buyers and carried to Havre, to Antwerp, to Bordeaux, meeting on the way other corn, from Odessa or Hamburg or New York, which was also earning for merchants, ship-owners and other harpies, immense profits, exorbitant freights, huge commissions...In other words, you sent away a quarter of wheat at 50 shillings, and got it back, if you got it at all, at 80 shillings.' (The Nation, 12 June 1847.)

The issue of food exports from Ireland during the famine remains a controversial aspect of the crisis as a whole. The traditional, populist view has considered the export of food to be a major contributory factor to excess mortality, signifying a triumph of doctrine over humanitarian considerations. The opposing interpretation has argued that even if all the food had been kept in Ireland, it was not sufficient to compensate for the shortfall resulting from the blight.

The 'debate' has tended to juxtapose the Young Irelander John Mitchel's emotive assertion regarding ships laden with food leaving Ireland against tabulations of the Irish grain trade in the 1840s, originally estimated by Austin Bourke. This is problematic, to say the least. By focusing almost exclusively on national estimates, there is little attempt to disaggregate the data by region or by product. The debate has confined itself to grain and thus the wider issue of food exports has been ignored. Equally, a net inflow of grain into Ireland in 1847 has to be viewed against the reality of a poor grain harvest in 1846. This meant that the volume of grain available for both home consumption and export had been much reduced anyway. Moreover, in looking at the issue of food exports, the role of ideology has been emphasised whilst financial motivations have been

30. John Mitchel (Currier and Ives).

underestimated. Another consequence of viewing this issue within such narrow parameters is that the role of Irish farmers and merchants, both individually and collectively, has been neglected.

The official returns compiled by the British Government of grain imports and exports are flawed. Apart from mistakes in computation and weight conversion, they are an under-representation of food exports from Ireland, so cannot provide a fully accurate gauge of food (or calorific) losses. The unreliability of the official data was a consequence of the Act of Union: Ireland was increasingly absorbed into a free-trade zone and there was little financial or fiscal necessity to keep accurate data of food imports from Ireland to Britain. Although overall estimates were made of grain imports from Ireland—upon which the British working classes relied so heavily—the returns were not comprehensive. Since 1825 the recording of all other foodstuffs by the central government had been discontinued, although records of live animal imports were kept intermittently. This lack of central attention makes research into local records even more important in understanding the impact of the famine.

Significant amounts of food were leaving Ireland during the famine years. In 1847 alone, the worst year of the Famine, almost 4,000 vessels carried food from Ireland to the major ports of Britain, such as Bristol, Glasgow, Liverpool and London. Over half of these ships went to Liverpool, the main port both for emigration and for cargo. Shipping returns for all of these vessels and full details of their cargoes have survived, although they have been little used (similar records for Ireland do not survive). Food was also exported to smaller ports such as Preston and Runcorn, although their records were not kept systematically. But those port records that do survive can throw new light on the question of food exports during the famine, while also providing an insight into the nature of the Irish economy in the 1840s.

By the 1840s, Ireland had become the granary of Britain, supplying the grain-hungry market with food sufficient to feed two million people annually. Grain was not the only major food export to Britain: the data suggests that at the time of the famine the population of Britain depended heavily on Ireland for a wide range of foodstuffs, and not just grain. At the same time, large quantities of other merchandise were exported from Ireland. In the twelve month period following the second failure of the potato crop in 1846, exports from Ireland included horses and ponies (over 4,000), bones, lard, animal skins, honey, tongues, rags, shoes, soap, glue and seed. This vast export trade suggests the diversity of the Irish economy during these years and how disease and starvation existed side-by-side with a substantial commercial sector.

Food cargoes were coming from ports throughout Ireland, not just on the east coast. Ports situated in some of the most famine-stricken parts of Ireland were sending cargoes of foodstuffs to Britain: Ballina, Ballyshannon, Bantry, Dingle, Killala, Kilrush, Limerick, Sligo, Tralee and Westport. In the first nine months

31. Food supplies under military escort, *Pictorial Times*, 30 October 1847.
(Guildhall Library, London)

of 1847, for example, seventy-five ships sailed from Tralee to Liverpool, most of
which were carrying grain. In the same period, six vessels sailed from Kilrush
in County Clare (which suffered acutely during the Famine) to Glasgow carrying a total of 6,624 barrels of oats. Throughout 1847 also, both Indian corn and
potatoes were exported from Ireland.

The question of free trade during a subsistence crisis lay at the heart of an
ongoing ideological battle within British politics. This was most evident in the
decision not to close Irish ports in response to food scarcity. It also demonstrated the political muscle of interest groups, but especially merchants, within
both Britain and Ireland. The closure of ports was a traditional, short-term
response to food shortages. It had been used to great effect during the subsistence crisis of 1782-84 when, despite the opposition of the grain merchants,
ports had been closed and bounties offered to merchants who imported food
to the country. During the subsistence crisis of 1799-1800, the government
had placed a temporary embargo on the export of potatoes from Ireland. In
1816 and 1821, the British Government had organised the shipment of grain
into areas in the west of Ireland where there were food shortages. The grain
was then sold on at low prices. Similar intervention and market regulation
occurred in Britain. For example, following the poor grain harvest in 1773,
the bounty on wheat exports was removed in an attempt to keep grain in the
country.

By the 1840s, this level of intervention was viewed by the government as being ideologically inappropriate as they preferred to leave food exports unhampered. In 1845 and 1846 there were calls from the corporations of Belfast, Cork, Derry, Dublin and Limerick for the ports to be closed in an effort to keep food in the country. At the same time, local and central governments throughout Europe were responding to food shortages in their own countries by closing their ports as a short-term expedient. The Dutch Government also repealed their Corn Laws in 1846 in an attempt to facilitate the import of cheap grain.

Sir Robert Peel had alienated his protectionist colleagues through his support for the repeal of the Corn Laws in 1846. He had also angered many Irish merchants by his decision to import Indian corn into Ireland following the first appearance of potato blight in 1845. A key aspect of Peel's relief programme had been that £100,000 of Indian corn from America was imported into Ireland in the spring and summer of 1846. The purpose of importing this was not primarily to provide food to the destitute, but to regulate and stabilise food prices within Ireland. This policy was successful and there was no excess mortality in 1845-46. The fall of Peel's government in the summer of 1846 brought the Whigs under Lord John Russell to power. The Whigs were even more divided on this matter, although the free-trade lobby within the party was very influential, especially following the 1847 general election.

A more controversial aspect of the policy of the Whig Government in 1846 was their decision not to continue Peel's policy of importing Indian corn to Ireland but to leave food importation to market forces, despite the fact that the shortfall in food supply was far higher than in the previous year. This decision was due to a mixture of ideological and practical considerations. Peel's intervention in the market place in 1845 had angered many merchants and grain producers. One of the first actions of the new administration was to assure this powerful interest group that only a limited number of government food depots would be opened in the west of Ireland, in the regions most badly affected by the famine. Instead, food imports were to be left to the workings of the market. Inevitably, merchants were tempted to seek high profits outside Ireland and the food shortages in the rest of Europe, including Britain, ensured that there was a ready market for their goods.

The destitute, whose existence depended on the vagaries of the free market economy, were untouched by the rising profits of the Irish merchants. This fact was recognised privately by a number of members of the government. At the beginning of 1847, when excess mortality was at its highest, the Lord Lieutenant, Bessborough, criticised the actions of the merchants. He believed that their behaviour and desire for high profits had contributed to the suffering as they had 'done their best to keep up prices'. He went on to reflect that 'I cannot make up my mind entirely about the merchants. I know all the difficulties that arise when you begin to interfere with trade, but it is difficult to persuade

32. Sir Robert Peel.

33. Lord John Russell and his cabinet discontinued the import of Indian meal into Ireland. (*Illustrated London News*)

a starving population that one class should be permitted to make 50 per cent profit by the sale of provisions whilst they are dying in want of these'.

At the end of 1845, exports of potatoes from Ireland increased, especially to England, Belgium and Holland, all of which had experienced the potato blight. The reduction of potatoes in the Irish markets caused some concern within Ireland, although overseas demand for Irish potatoes diminished when some of them arrived at their ports of destination diseased with blight. The export of livestock to Britain (with the exception of pigs) also increased during the famine. Whilst the export of pigs decreased, the export of bacon and ham increased from 930 cwt. in 1846 to 1,061 cwt. in 1847. In total over three million live animals were exported between 1846-50, more than the number of people who emigrated during the famine years. In 1847, 9,992 calves were exported from Ireland to Britain, which represented a thirty-three per cent increase on exports on the previous year. Some of these cattle were then re-exported to Europe. Overall, during the famine years, food exports to Europe from Britain increased. Irish food exports, however, went much further afield than Britain or even Europe. In the summer of 1847, a New York newspaper noted that imports of grain from Ireland were even larger than usual.

A wide variety of other foodstuffs left Ireland apart from livestock—vegetables and pulses (particularly peas, beans and onions), dairy products, fish (especially salmon, oysters and herrings) and even rabbits. In February 1847, 377 boxes of 'fish and eggs' and 383 boxes of fish were imported into Bristol alone. The butter export trade was particularly buoyant. In the first week of 1847, for example, 4,455 firkins of butter (a firkin equals nine gallons) were exported from Ireland to Liverpool. In the following week, this had risen to 4,691 firkins. Large quantities of butter were exported from Cork to all parts of Britain. For example, in the first nine months of 1847, 56,557 firkins of butter were exported to Bristol and 34,852 firkins to Liverpool. During the same period, 3,435 poultry were exported to Liverpool and 2,375 to Bristol.

Alcohol was also a major export item. Although the foundation of Father Mathew's temperance movement in 1838 had damaged the Irish alcoholic drink industry, it remained an important sector of the economy both for internal and external consumption. In 1847, six million gallons of grain spirit were consumed within Ireland. Exports were also high, mostly in the form of ale, stout, porter, and whiskey. These products were derived from grain (barley and malt or, to a limited extent, potatoes) and thus represented a disguised export of grain. In the first nine months of 1847, for example, 874,170 gallons of porter were exported from Ireland to Liverpool. During the same period, 278,658 gallons of Guinness were imported into Bristol. Whiskey exports were also substantial and 183,392 gallons of this spirit arrived in Liverpool alone. This aspect of the export trade was criticised within Ireland. The prohibition of distillation during a subsistence crisis was a traditional response by governments. In both 1845 and 1846, there were calls for distillation to be outlawed. This included requests from the corporation of Dublin and the Lord Lieutenant, Lord Heytesbury. These entreaties were refused.

In spite of the apparent commitment of both Peel and Russell's governments to free trade, imports and exports continued to be hampered by the Navigation Acts, which restricted the ability of foreign ships to carry goods to ports in the United Kingdom. At the same time, freight charges were imposed on goods imported into the United Kingdom. These charges were highly volatile and, after the disastrous harvest of 1846, rose to three times their usual rate. This body of legislation and the continuation of freight charges hindered the free movement of goods into Ireland, especially during the critical months in the winter of 1846-47. This was recognised by the barrister Isaac Butt, who was formerly Professor of Political Economy at Trinity College, Dublin. In 1847, he identified the paradox of expecting free trade to supply the Irish market whilst trade continued to be hampered by various restrictions. This led him to pose the rhetorical question that, 'if ministers resolved to trust the lives of the Irish people to private enterprise, was it not common sense and common justice to them that private enterprise should be unencumbered by any restrictions in the execution of the task of supplying, at the notice of a few months, provisions to five million people'?

By January 1847 it was obvious that the relief policies introduced by the Whig administration only a few months earlier had failed. In an attempt to ameliorate the situation, the government announced that the public works were to be replaced by soup kitchens. Furthermore, the Navigation Acts and all duties on foreign grain were temporarily suspended. These measures undoubtedly facilitated imports into Ireland in the spring and summer of 1847, when grain imports began to rise sharply and food prices to fall. This legislation coincided with the closing of the public works programme and their replacement with government soup kitchens, which were highly successful. However, these measures were too late to help the hundreds of thousands of people who had died in the preceding winter months when there had been a clear starvation gap for the destitute of Ireland. During these months, deprivation and starvation co-existed with a thriving export trade and high profit margins, demonstrating the duality of the Irish economy.

The second failure of the potato crop in 1846 left many people without access to their usual supply of food. The Whig Government's decision not to intervene in the market place but to use public works as the main means of providing relief was disastrous. In many instances, the wages paid on the relief works proved to be too low to purchase food in a period of 'famine' prices, forestalling and hoarding. At the same time, large amounts of food continued to leave Ireland and it was not until the following spring that food imports became substantial. Consequently, during the winter, there was a 'starvation gap'. The size of that gap is best measured, not in calorific values or in terms of the volume of food exported, but in the amount of excess mortality and suffering during those months. Whilst official mortality statistics were not kept, the local Irish constabulary provided an unofficial estimate that 400,000 people had died due to a lack of food in the winter of 1846-47.

The belief that the British Government had abandoned the Irish destitute to market forces was not confined to nationalists such as John Mitchel. The Earl of Clarendon, who had succeeded Bessborough as Lord Lieutenant, confided to the Prime Minister at the end of 1847 that 'no-one could now venture to dispute the fact that Ireland had been sacrificed to the London corn-dealers because you were a member for the City, and that no distress would have occurred if the exportation of Irish grain had been prohibited'.

Chapter 8

'The Widow's Mite':
Private relief during the Great Famine

Christine Kinealy

During previous food shortages in Ireland, including those of 1822 and 1831, charitable bodies had been set up to provide relief at a local level, and some of these were revived following the first failure of the potato crop in 1845. But after 1846 donations came from all over the world, even from people who had no connection with Ireland. This help cut across religious, national and economic differences. It came from people who were themselves poor, including former slaves in the Caribbean, Native Americans and prisoners in Britain. Heads of states were also involved—Queen Victoria, the sultan of the Ottoman Empire, and the president of the United States. Extensive fund-raising was carried out in Ireland by all sections of society. Resident landlords were generally involved, although many absentees were criticised for their indifference. Even children raised funds: for example, pupils in a school in Armagh City collected for the local poor in 1847.

Traditionally, Irish landlords have generally been condemned for their callous attitude towards their poor tenants. In fact, their responses varied; while some used the distress to evict their tenants, others gave relief in different ways. When the blight came a second time, some landlords lowered their rents by ten per cent. These actions tended to be short-term, especially because landowners themselves had financial problems when rates (local taxes) rose steeply and income from rents fell.

Most of the charitable efforts of Irish landlords were concentrated on the early months of 1847. The marquis of Sligo, a liberal landlord, was chairman of a committee that set up a private soup kitchen in Westport in January 1847. He made an initial donation of £100 and promised a subscription of £5 per week. Other local gentry and Church of Ireland clergy contributed, and the opening fund reached £255. In County Down Lord Roden, a landlord known for his evangelical views and his involvement in the Orange Order, opened a soup shop on his estate where soup, made of rice and meal porridge, was sold at a penny a quart and potato cake cost a penny for 12oz. Some landlords, such as the earl of Shannon, also resold soup at less than cost. In Skibbereen, which became infamous for the sufferings of its people, the Church of Ireland minister, Revd Caulfield, was giving 1,149 people one free pint of soup each day. In Belfast a privately funded relief committee in Ballymacarrett gave soup to over 12,000 people daily, about 60 per cent of the local (predominantly Protestant) population. On some estates rent was reduced or employment provided. Daniel O'Connell reduced rents on his County Kerry property by 50 per cent. Lord and Lady Waterford financed a soup kitchen on their estate, and Maria Edgeworth in Edgeworthstown provided free seed to her tenants. The earl of Devon sent £2,000 and the duke of Devonshire £100 to help their tenants. But not all landlords were generous. The absentee landlord James Robinson donated only £1 to the Waterford Union for its soup kitchen. Lord Londonderry, one of the ten richest men in the United Kingdom, who owned land in counties Down, Derry, Donegal and Antrim in addition to property in Britain, was criticised for his meanness: he and his wife gave £30 to the local relief committee but spent £150,000 renovating their Irish home.

The famine also attracted assistance from a wide variety of religious congregations and communities at home and overseas, ranging from Hindus in India to Jews and Baptists in New York. In Ireland, the Society of Friends (Quakers, as discussed by Rob Goodbody below) distinguished itself by its relief efforts. The larger churches also played an important part in the distribution of both government and private relief. Local priests and ministers were widely praised for their role in helping the poor, and some established their own relief committees

34. *The Eviction*, by Erskine Nicol, 1853. (National Gallery of Ireland)

to raise funds. Two Catholic bishops, Archbishop Daniel Murray of Dublin and Archbishop John MacHale of Tuam, were particularly prominent in organising relief. Catholic aid continued beyond 1847, when many other forms of private relief had ceased. The amount collected is hard to quantify but it was probably more than £400,000, which was distributed by local priests, thus avoiding much of the expense and delay that marked government relief.

The Irish Catholic Church used its overseas network to attract donations, with large sums being raised in Britain and the United States. *The Tablet*, the leading English Catholic newspaper, offered to act as a channel for English Catholics to send money. By March 1847 Bishop John Fitzpatrick in Boston had raised almost $20,000, mostly from local Catholics, though it was meant for distribution to all creeds in Ireland. The staff and students of Maynooth College made a donation of over £200.

A committee for the Irish poor was established in Rome on 13 January 1847. Pope Pius IX donated 1,000 Roman crowns from his own pocket. In addition to personal financial assistance, he offered practical support. In March 1847 he took the unprecedented step of issuing a papal encyclical to the international Catholic community, appealing for support for the victims of the famine. As a result, large sums of money were raised by Catholic congregations: the Society of Vincent de Paul in France raised £5,000; the diocese of Strasbourg collected 23,365 francs; two priests in Caracas in Venezuela contributed £177; one Father Fahy in Argentina sent over £600; a priest in Grahamstown, South Africa, donated £70; and the Catholic community in Sydney, New South Wales, sent £1,500. Despite the unique intervention by Pope Pius IX, the Irish bishops failed to thank him for his donation or for the encyclical letter until forced to do so by Dr Paul Cullen. Cardinal Giacomo Fransoni, an adviser to the pope, even accused the Irish bishops of laziness in fund-raising for the poor, even though he had given them official permission to do whatever needed to be done. The thanklessness of the Irish bishops and their wrangling with one another lost them further vital support in Rome. The pope's concern and support for Ireland came to an abrupt end in 1848, when the revolutionary struggle in Italy forced him to flee Rome. Nevertheless, his brief interest had a major effect in encouraging the international Catholic community to support relief in Ireland. But things could be difficult. As the experience of the bishop of Augsburg demonstrated, transferring money to Ireland could be complicated.

Women, who were generally invisible in public affairs, were particularly involved in the collection and distribution of private relief. They were encouraged by the early action of Queen Victoria, who donated £2,000 to the British Relief Association in January 1847. This made her the largest single donor to famine relief. More importantly, Victoria published two 'Queen's Letters', the first in March 1847 and the second in October 1847, asking people in Britain to donate money to relieve Irish distress. The first was printed in the main

NOTICE

TO

THE EARL OF CHARLEMONT'S TENANTRY.

IN consideration of the extensive failure in the POTATO CROP this Season, willing to bear his share in the general calamity, and anxious to relieve, as far as in him lies, his Poorer Tenants from an undue share of suffering under the Divine Will, LORD CHARLEMONT has directed that the following Scale of Reduction, in Payment of Rent, shall be adopted for this Year, upon his Estates in the COUNTIES of ARMAGH and TYRONE, viz.:—

25 per Cent. on Rents under £5	10 per Cent. on Rents under £20.
20 per Cent. on Rents under £10	5 per Cent. on Rents under £30.
15 per Cent. on Rents under £15	No Discount on Rents exceeding £30.

Abatements, according to the above Scale, shall be made only to Tenants holding under Lease paying the present Annual value; and Tenants-at-will, not being occupiers of Town Parks, upon their paying the Year's Rent now in course of Collection, on or before the days appointed underneath:—

ALTATYLE, AUGHNACLOY, ANAGHA, & ANAGHMACMANUS,	On Tuesday, 3d Nov., 1846.	GRANGEBLUNDELS,...... GRANEMORE.............. GRANGEMORE,..........	On Wednesday, 25th November, 1846.
AUGHMAGORGAN,........ BALLYLEAN,............	On Wednesday, 4th November, 1846.		
BALLYMACNABB,......... BALLYBRANNAN,........ BALLYMACAULLY,........	On Tuesday, 10th November, 1846.	KILLMAKEW,.............. KILLMAKEW,.............. DRUMMONBEG,.......... LURGABOY,............	On Tuesday, 1st December, 1846.
CARRICKATOAL,......... CARNAVANAGHAN,...... CAVANAGROUGH,........	On Wednesday, 11th November, 1846.	LARAGH ASHANKILL,..... MAGHERY................ RATHDRUMGRANA....... TASSAGH,................	On Wednesday, 2d December, 1846.
CASHILL, ... CLADYMORE,..............	On Saturday, 14th November, 1846.		
CLADYBEG,............... CLOGHFIN,................ CREEVEROE,..............	On Tuesday, 17th November, 1846.	TIRNASCOBE,.............. TYREARLY,................ TULLYSARRIN,............	On Tuesday, 8th December, 1846.
CORR and DONAVALLEY... CORCLEA,................	On Wednesday, 18th November, 1846.	DRUMCART,............... DRUMGRANNON,......... LISROAN,................	On Wednesday, 9th December, 1846.
DAMELLY,................ DRUMATEE,.............. DRUMACHEE,............	On Saturday, 21st November, 1846.		
DERRYLARD,............. FOLEY,.................... ENAGH,...................	On Tuesday, 24th November, 1846.	LISTAMNET,............... MOY,..................... TYRLEENAN,..............	On Saturday, 12th December, 1846.

*** Where a Tenant is subject to the payment of more than One Rent, the abatement shall be made according to the Gross Annual Amount to which he is liable.

☞ Where Two or more Occupiers hold under one Lease, the Total Rent reserved by the Lease shall be taken as the sum to regulate the per Centage to be allowed.

W. W. ALGEO.

ARMAGH, 13th October, 1846.
ARMAGH—PRINTED BY J. M'W...

35. Rent abatement notice in 1846 from the earl of Charlemont to his tenants in counties Armagh and Tyrone. In folk memory, Irish landlords generally have been condemned for their callous attitude. In fact, the response varied; while some used the distress to evict their tenants, others gave relief in different ways, often in the form of rent abatements, as here. (National Library of Ireland)

36. By January 1847 this Society of Friends soup kitchen in Cork was distributing 6,800 litres daily. (*Illustrated London News*)

newspapers and read out in Anglican churches. Following its publication, a proclamation announced that 24 March 1847 had been chosen as a day for a 'General Fast and Humiliation before Almighty God', and the proceeds were to be distributed to Ireland and Scotland. The Queen's first letter raised £170,571, but the second raised only £30,167. In fact, the second letter was widely condemned in Britain, indicating a hardening in public attitudes towards the giving of private relief to Ireland.

Following the second appearance of the blight in 1846, associations such as the Ladies' Relief Association in Dublin and the Belfast Ladies' Association were formed. The Society of Friends also established separate ladies' committees. One of the most successful of the women's groups was the Belfast Ladies' Association, which first met on 1 January 1847. The oldest member was Mary Ann McCracken (the sister of the United Irishman Henry Joy McCracken, who was executed as a rebel in 1798). Initially the association was formed for the relief of distressed districts in the west of the country, but increasingly it became clear that there was famine elsewhere, even in industrial towns such as Belfast, and so their involvement became nationwide. Apart from food and clothes, they provided poor women with wool and flax to enable them to

37. Jonathan Pim, joint secretary of the Central Relief Committee of the Society
of Friends. He later collapsed from overwork. (Friends Historical Library)

work. This Committee refused to proselytise, that is, convert poor Catholics to
Protestantism in exchange for relief.

Some ladies' groups did proselytise, however, including the Belfast Ladies'
Association for Connaught. They wanted to counteract the effects of the famine
in the west of Ireland by trying to 'improve, by industry, the temporal condition of the poor of the females of Connaught and their spiritual [condition] by
the truth of the Bible'. These aims had support from both evangelical clergy

38. Queen Victoria, pilloried in folk memory as the 'Famine Queen' who only donated £5 in famine relief, in fact donated £2,000 to the British Relief Association in January 1847, making her the largest single donor. (Multitext Project)

and politicians. By 1849 the Association had collected £15,000 and established industrial schools in 'wild Connaught', where skills such as knitting and needle-work were taught. By 1850, thirty-two schoolmistresses were employed within the province, who worked under the direction of the resident ladies. In the same year the association claimed to have offered employment and education to over 2,000 poor girls and women. Its members tried to change the habits and moral-ity of the poor in general by influencing the behaviour of women.

A remarkably diverse range of activities were undertaken by women of all denominations. Food kitchens were set up; women organised the distribution of relief and collected money; nuns nursed in fever hospitals and fed the starv-ing at their convents. Women tried practical solutions to poverty by creating employment for the female poor in cottage industries. Generally, this work depended on the enthusiasm of individuals. Needlework became an integral part of the education given by nuns to poor children, and many laywomen acted as teachers and benefactors in schools where needlework was taught. Similar work was carried out by the Ladies' Industrial Society of Ireland, founded at the height of the famine in 1847 to 'carry out a system for encouraging and developing the latent capacities of the poor of Ireland'. Other smaller ladies' committees were formed, such as the Newry Benevolent Female Working Society, which provided employment for women in spinning, knitting and needlework.

The United States, which had strong connections with Ireland, provided very significant private relief—in excess of $2,000,000. A large part was in the form of cash, food, clothing and blankets. One of the first relief committees was established in Boston at the end of 1845, although most of the relief efforts came after the second failure of the potato crop in 1846. The Boston committee, which included many members of the local Repeal Association, blamed the Famine on British misrule. There was a more widespread response to the second potato failure, helped by the fact that the United States had enjoyed a bumper harvest. An attempt was even made by the US Senate to provide $500,000 for Irish relief, though it ultimately failed. Nonetheless, in 1847, members of the American Government, including the vice-president, George Dallas, were giving assistance to Ireland. The president, James Polk, made a $50 donation: a Boston newspaper declared scornfully that it was too small and had to be 'squeezed' out of him.

By January 1847 the payments totalled over a million dollars. One action of the relief committees in Boston that received great publicity was the sending of two ships (the *Jamestown* and the *Macedonian*) full of supplies to Cork in 1847. The *Jamestown* completed the journey to Cobh in record time. A portion of the food on the *Macedonian* was distributed in Scotland. Both ships were manned by volunteers. The fact that the United States was in the middle of a war with Mexico made its government's granting of permission more noteworthy. In reply to criticisms for permitting a US warship to be used for the benefit of another country, Captain Forbes of the *Jamestown* declared that 'it is not an everyday matter to see a nation starving'. A Boston newspaper described the mission of the *Jamestown* as 'one of the most sublime transactions in the nation's history'. Some Cork newspapers used its arrival to contrast the generosity of the United States with the meanness of the British Government. In total, over 100 vessels carrying 20,000 tons of foodstuffs came from the United States to Ireland in the wake of the *Jamestown*.

Although many high-ranking officials became involved in relief, donations also came from people who were themselves poor and disadvantaged, such as the Native American Choctaw nation of Oklahoma. Their contribution of $170 was made through the American Society of Friends. Prisoners in Sing Sing Jail also made a donation. Jacob Harvey, who coordinated relief donations in New York, estimated that in January and February 1846, Irish labourers and servants had sent $326,410 to Ireland in small bank drafts.

Assistance came from unexpected places. The first famine subscription had been raised in India at the end of 1845, on the initiative of British troops serving in Calcutta. It was followed by the formation of the Indian Relief Fund in January 1846, which appealed to British people living in India to start similar collections. They raised almost £14,000. The Freemasons of India contributed

39. US President James Polk made a $50 donation: a Boston newspaper declared scornfully that it was too small and had to be 'squeezed' out of him. (Tennessee Historical Society)

40. The USS *Macedonian* arrived at Cork with food aid from New York in summer 1847. Local newspapers used the occasion to contrast the generosity of the United States with the meanness of the British Government. (*Illustrated London News*)

£5,000. A contribution of £3,000 was raised in Bombay in one week. The government of Barbados gave a donation, partly inspired by one received from Ireland some years earlier. In 1847–8, committees in Australia raised over £10,000. Money was set aside to assist emigration from Ireland to Australia, but was eventually returned to the donors because the committee could not agree about the kind of emigrants to help, whether paupers or able-bodied emigrants. Other donations came from South Africa (£550), St Petersburg, Russia (£2,644), Constantinople (£620), the islands of Seychelles and Rodrigues (£111 and £16) and Mexico (£652). This shows that the famine had become an event of international significance.

Private charities provided essential relief, but the activities of a few were controversial, especially where they were associated with proselytism. In the genuine belief that they were saving souls, a small number of Protestant evangelicals used the hunger of Catholics as a means to convert them. The converts were given disparaging names: 'soupers', 'jumpers' or 'perverts'. A few charitable bodies read the Bible to the poor to whom they gave food. In the west of Ireland, famine missionaries, such as the evangelicals Revd Hyacinth Talbot D'Arcy and Revd Edward Nangle, tried to win converts in this way. Some evangelicals believed that the British Government had caused the famine by giving a grant to Maynooth College in 1845 to train Catholic priests.

Another well-known missionary who worked in the west of Ireland was Michael Brannigan, a convert from Catholicism to Presbyterianism and a fluent Irish speaker. In 1847 he established twelve schools in counties Mayo and Sligo, and by the end of 1848 the number had grown to 28, despite 'priestly opposition'. Attendance dropped when the British Relief Association began providing each child with a half-pound of corn-meal every day, but this ended on 15 August 1848 when funds ran out.

The worries of the Catholic Church are well put in a letter from Fr William Flannelly of Ballinakill, County Galway, to Archbishop Murray of Dublin, on 6 April 1849: 'It cannot be wondered if a starving people would be perverted in shoals, especially as they [the missionaries] go from cabin to cabin, and when they find the inmates naked and starved to death, they proffer food, money and raiment, on the express condition of becoming members of their conventicles'. The *Freeman's Journal* condemned this as 'nefarious unchristian wickedness'. The pope felt worried enough to urge the Catholic hierarchy to oppose the work of missionaries and, on one occasion, he reprimanded the bishops for not doing enough to protect their flocks.

By 1851 the main missions claimed that they had won 35,000 converts and they were anxious to win more. Shortly afterwards, 100 additional preachers were sent to Ireland by the Protestant Alliance. Well-provisioned missionary settlements in such destitute areas as Dingle and Achill Island attracted many converts. The missions were generally opposed by the Church of Ireland, but their impact was, in the end, slight and tended to be localised. Some charitable organisations (including orders of nuns) believed that the distress gave them an opportunity to teach the Irish peasantry 'good' habits of hard work. The missions, and the illiberal reaction of the Catholic clergy, tended to encourage sectarianism. Besides, many converts had to go elsewhere because of hostility and contempt in their own communities.

Most private donations and charitable bodies came to an end at the harvest of 1847, partly because donations had started to dry up, but also because the blight had not appeared in 1847 and people believed, tragically, the famine was over. Though private charity during the crisis was short-lived, it played a vital role in saving lives.

Chapter 9

Quakers and the famine

Rob Goodbody

When the potato crop failed once again due to blight in 1846 it was obvious, in Ireland at any rate, that a major catastrophe was about to occur. Members of the Society of Friends (Quakers) were amongst those who understood the seriousness of the situation and many of them reacted by setting up relief operations in their own areas. In the autumn of 1846 soup kitchens were set up by Quakers in towns such as Waterford, Enniscorthy, Limerick, Clonmel and Youghal. Any thought of setting up a more comprehensive relief programme was hampered by two drawbacks. First, the number of Quakers in Ireland was small—a mere 3,000 or so out of a population that exceeded eight million. Second, the Quaker population was concentrated in certain areas and was almost entirely absent from the west, including Donegal, Kerry, Clare, west Cork and the whole of Connaught. Quaker relief, therefore, could not be offered directly in the areas which would suffer most.

The Society of Friends had certain advantages, though, if the right method of providing relief could be found. Quakers had a well-developed network of committees which operated on a nationwide basis to organise their own society. Through these committees and through family ties Quakers throughout Ireland were in close contact with each other and with those in Britain. Many Irish Quakers were merchants and would have had the organisational capacity to purchase goods and move them efficiently to other parts of the country. Above all, Quakers believed that God was present in everyone and this gave an understanding that the individual in distress should be helped if at all possible.

It was with this in mind that a number of Quakers, led by the Dublin businessman Joseph Bewley, organised a meeting in November 1846. The outcome was the establishment of a twenty-one member 'central relief committee'. To facilitate frequent meetings membership was confined to the Dublin area, while a further group of twenty-one would be nominated as 'corresponding members' and from the Quaker community outside Dublin. Following discussions with their Irish counterparts Quakers in London also established a relief committee.

Throughout the famine these two committees worked closely together, with the Dublin committee looking after grants of food and clothing while the London committee raised funds. The division of labour was not strict, however, and many English Quakers came to Ireland to see for themselves just how bad the situation was and to become involved directly with the giving of relief. As the work of these committees progressed, they set up various subcommittees to handle specific tasks and amongst these were local committees in cities and towns such as Waterford, Cork, Limerick and Clonmel, which looked after relief operations in the south and south-west.

The first and most obvious means of assisting the hungry was through direct grants of food or the money with which food could be purchased. Some of this went to Quaker relief workers in the field, but the scope for this kind of aid was limited by the size and distribution of the Quaker community. A great deal more was done through assistance to non-Quakers who were running local relief efforts and through Quaker workers identifying local people who were capable of operating soup kitchens and encouraging them to become involved. In essence, the relief committees of the Society of Friends acted as intermediaries who encouraged those who had something to offer to donate it and then made these donations available to local activists. In their own words the Quaker workers provided a 'suitable channel' through which aid was brought from the donors to the recipients.

Before long the committees became involved in the distribution of clothing. In the winter of 1846-47 a large proportion of the clothing donations came from English committees, mostly consisting of women. Some clothes were made by the donors, while others came from factories as a result of pressure from the women's committees. A warehouse was taken in Dublin to receive donations and sort them into bundles for passing on to the destitute. In the following winter American donations were predominant and this was mostly in the form of fabrics so that employment could be generated in making clothing.

In the summer of 1847 there was a major change of direction in the type of relief offered by the Quaker committees. The emphasis on grants of food and clothing was greatly reduced in favour of longer-term means of assistance. There were many reasons for this. First, there was a change in the type of relief offered by the government: soup kitchens were established by the Poor Law Unions to feed the destitute without admitting them to the workhouse. The Quakers recognised that there was going to be a hiatus following the closure of the public works schemes and before the Poor Law Unions could set up the soup kitchens. They ensured that their own relief efforts were kept going to bridge that gap as far as they could manage, but once the government soup kitchens were established they saw no point in duplicating them.

Second, the Quaker relief committees were suffering from both donor fatigue and physical fatigue. In essence, their operations had been established to meet the shortages expected in 1846-47 and many of the donors had given all that they could afford. The resources of the relief committees had been carefully managed over the year, but there was a comparatively small amount left by the summer of 1847. With the co-operation of the government a survey was carried out among the officials who ran the poor law unions, which showed that the magnitude of the destitution was so great that the resources of the Quaker committees could not even scratch the surface of what was required. Their original assertion was that 'if there be 1000 of our fellow men who would perish if nothing be done, our rescue of 100 from destruction is surely not the less a duty and a privilege, because there are another 900 whom we cannot save'. In theory this maxim should remain valid if the proportion was 100 out of hundreds of thousands, but in practice the resources available might not have saved anyone at all given the scale of the destitution.

Instead, it was felt that meagre resources should be kept only for those who were not eligible for government assistance and for longer-term projects. Members of the Society of Friends had always felt that the only way to make a lasting contribution to help solve the problem was by means other than short-term distribution of food. The first moves towards this type of aid came in the early days of the Quaker involvement when cash donations were given to people in Galway and Mayo who had set up local employment schemes, mainly involved with weaving and other textile production. As time went on, however, a greater variety of projects were undertaken or supported.

In a famine it is a natural reaction to seek alternative ways of producing food and Quaker workers sought to do this through assistance to fisheries. In the early stages of the relief efforts, Quaker travellers in Galway City discovered that the fishermen of the nearby Claddagh had pawned their nets and other equipment during the previous year and were destitute. Through cash loans the tackle was redeemed and the fishing community became self-sufficient again. Similar aid was given to fishermen in such coastal towns as Kingstown, Arklow and Ballycotton and for a small initial input poverty-stricken communities were given back the means of supporting themselves. In the main the loans were repaid within a short time and the funds became available again for other purposes.

Not content with helping existing fishing communities, the Quaker committees became involved in projects to foster new fisheries. For a variety of reasons these were not successful—distance from markets and the lack of bait due to the destruction of shellfish beds by the starving population. Fishery projects at Achill and Ballinakill Bay, near Clifden in County Galway, did not last long. Another, at Belmullet in County Mayo, kept going for two years from the end of 1847 and some fifteen fishing boats and ten curraghs were fitted out. Ultimately this project failed through bad management by the proprietor. A fourth project was undertaken at Castletownbere in west Cork from the autumn of 1847, lasting for nearly five years and employing fifty-four men and boys. Eventually this, too, failed through bad management. Probably the most worthwhile fishery project was that which was established at Ring in County Waterford through the initiative of the local Church of Ireland vicar and which was given financial support by the Quaker relief committee based in Waterford itself. This provided work and food for a number of families and for a time a fish-curing plant was operated here with Quaker funding.

In the spring of 1847 an English Quaker, William Bennett, arrived in Ireland with the intention of touring the worst-hit areas. He believed that as the potato had proved to be an unreliable source of food there was a need to encourage a greater diversity of crops. To this end he and his son acquired seed from W. Drummond and Sons in Dawson Street. His main choice was turnip seed together with carrots and mangelwurzel, and later he included cabbage, parsnip and flax. Bennett distributed most of his seed in Mayo and Donegal and while he was there he also made cash grants to local craft industries that had been set up to provide employment. After six weeks he returned to England where he published a book entitled *Six Weeks in Ireland*, which was influential in encouraging the flow of donations.

Some of the local Quaker committees became involved in the distribution of seed but the central committee in Dublin was hesitant, believing that any crops grown would be distrained by the landlords in lieu of rent owed. However, in May 1847, Sir Randolph Routh, the government's Commissary-General, gave some eighteen tons of seed to the committee for distribution. The task of organising distribution was given to William Todhunter, who managed to do so by means of the postal system together with free carriage donated by a coach company and a steampacket company. Some 40,000 smallholders received grants of seed and it is estimated that 9,600 acres of crops were sown.

Following the success of this operation the Quaker central relief committee repeated the exercise in the spring of 1848, laying out an initial sum of £5,000 to purchase and distribute almost sixty tons of seed. It is estimated that 32,000 acres of crops were grown as a result and that about 150,000 people would have been supplied with food as a result. The next logical step after the distribution of seed was to become directly involved in agriculture. Members of the Society of Friends who were involved in the relief operations could see that the government relief works did nothing to improve the long term prospects of the country as they were mostly concentrated on non-productive tasks. In 1848 the idea of undertaking agricultural reclamation works was put forward as a more useful operation.

The initiative came from a group of landowners on the borders of counties Mayo and Sligo, near Ballina, who approached the central relief committee in the spring of 1848 with an offer of the free use of land for a season. The offer was taken up, some 550 Irish acres, equivalent to about 360 hectares, were selected for the scheme and more than 1000 people were taken on to prepare the land for crops using spade labour. The workers were paid by the task, but unlike the government works of the previous season, the rates of pay were higher than normal to allow for the lower productivity to be expected from people debilitated by the effects of famine and disease. The cost of this project was about £300 in a normal week, but reached £500 a week from time to time. Part of the cost was laid out in the purchase of fertiliser and care was taken to use only imported fertiliser to avoid distorting the local market and pricing it out of the reach of other farmers.

A variety of crops were sown and again the turnip formed a large part of the operation, while for obvious reasons no potatoes were sown. In order to bring some diversity of employment a certain quantity of flax was also introduced. However, when the harvest came this spade-cultivation experiment proved very disappointing in its yield. Various reasons were advanced for this, including the previous condition of the land, which seemed to be borne out when the landowners managed a far better yield in the following season. In all, however, the project was a success in its main two aims to provide employment and to teach small-holders how to manage alternative varieties of crops.

The central relief committee was also involved in a number of similar projects on smaller scales through the giving of loans for spade cultivation to local landowners. The success of these was often better than that of the Ballina project and in general the loans were repaid. A further benefit of the various agricultural schemes was the effect on the local economies. Some of the landowners involved in these projects commented that the numbers of people dependant on the local poor law unions had greatly decreased with a consequent reduction in the rates. One commentator in Fermanagh estimated that the poor law rate in the district where his spade cultivation scheme had operated was as little as 12 per cent of the local average.

Following the experience in Ballina, a proposal was put forward to the central relief committee that it should establish a model farm for the more effective teaching of methods of growing crops and to act as an example of how a well-run farm should operate. A suitable property was found at Colmanstown in east Galway in the spring of 1849 and an extensive range of farm buildings was constructed. Before the farm could become fully operational, a considerable amount of land reclamation was required and this involved the removal of ditches to create larger fields and the laying of land drains. A stream was diverted to supply water to a mill which would carry out the threshing and milling of the grain crops. Some 228 people were employed on the Colmanstown model farm and a variety of crops was grown including grain and green crops, while there was also a wide range of farm animals such as cattle, sheep and pigs. This project was continued long after the end of the famine, only coming to an end in the early 1860s when the property was sold.

In line with the belief that longer-term changes were needed, the Quaker relief operation sought to encourage the diversification of the economy and this included various industrial projects. An attempt was made in 1848 to become directly involved through the establishment of a flannel manufacturing operation in Connaught. While the project was considered to be worthwhile and machinery was found for the task, at a late stage the committee shied away from direct involvement, deciding instead to offer financial backing to any suitable person who wished to take on the enterprise. Unfortunately, no one came forward.

A number of loans and grants were given to others who were providing industrial employment, ranging from small-scale cottage industries to factory or mill-based enterprises. Amongst the latter were flax mills set up in the Ballina area as a direct result of the Quaker spade-cultivation exercise in 1848.

The Society of Friends was in frequent contact with the government and in a number of ways these contacts were useful and successful. In the early stages the London committee persuaded the government to make available two steamships to bring supplies collected in Britain over to the west coast of Ireland. A little later the government was prevailed upon to pay the considerable cost of transporting American food across the Atlantic. A major operational cost within Ireland could have been the transport and storage of food, but an agreement with the government commissariat removed the cost and responsibility entirely. Under this arrangement all food landed in Ireland for the Quaker relief operations would be handed over directly to the commissariat in exchange for a credit note. This note could be used at any commissariat depot throughout Ireland to draw down supplies of food for distribution locally.

The London relief committee succeeded in persuading the Admiralty to update the charts of the west coast of Ireland as the existing charts had proved to be extremely inaccurate and useless for fisheries. Other campaigns undertaken included lobbying to have restrictions on fishing relaxed to improve the amount of food available. The greatest of these campaigns was the attempt to persuade the government to make fundamental changes in the system of land tenure. Much of this work was carried out by Jonathan Pim, one of the secretaries of the Dublin committee. He published a book on the subject in 1848 and he had a part in the final drafting of the Encumbered Estates Act of 1849. Long after the famine was over Pim continued his campaign for land reform and in 1865 he entered parliament as a member for Dublin. It is likely that he was heavily involved in the drafting of later land acts, even after he had left parliament.

When the central relief committee published its report in 1852 it concluded that its famine operations had not been a success. In the context of the time this was the only possible conclusion as no organisation could celebrate the success of a relief operation in the light of the massive toll of death and emigration.

Looked at another way, however, this cannot be deemed a failure. The extent and variety of the Friends' relief operations were out of proportion to the mere 3,000 members of the Society in Ireland. The total of £200,000 that was handled by the Quaker relief bodies was a small part of the total from all sources, but it nevertheless represents about £11 million at today's prices. Nearly 8,000 tons of food were distributed along with almost 300 soup boilers and nearly 80 tons of seed. Countless numbers of people were given employment in agriculture, fisheries and industry and many more were taught how to grow crops which had previously been unfamiliar to them. While the relief was organised by a religious body there was a strict rule that there were to be no religious strings attached.

The exercise was not without its toll among the Quaker relief workers. The strain of intense involvement over a protracted period affected the health of many workers and some died. Others contracted famine diseases in the course of their relief works. It is not known how many died either directly or indirectly as a result of their involvement, but the few who are known include Joseph Bewley, the leading light in the Dublin operations, who died of a heart attack at the age of fifty-six through over-work. Jacob Harvey, who was central to the operations in New York, also died through over-exertion as did William Todhunter, who was aged forty-six. Abraham Beale of the Cork committee contracted typhus and died.

The selfless way in which these Quakers gave of their time, energies and even their health made an enduring impact on their reputation and to this day the famine relief efforts of the Society of Friends have not been forgotten in Irish views of the Great Famine.

Chapter 10

Epidemic diseases of the Great Famine

Laurence M. Geary

Famine can be defined as a failure of food production or distribution, resulting in dramatically increased mortality. In Ireland between 1845 and 1849, general starvation and disease were responsible for more than 1,000,000 excess deaths, most of them attributable to fever, dysentery and small-pox. These three highly contagious diseases, which had long been endemic in Ireland, swept through the country. Their destructiveness was intensified by the presence of other epidemic infections, especially tuberculosis, bronchitis, influenza, pneumonia, diarrhoea and measles. The arrival of Asiatic cholera as a pandemic in 1848-49 exacerbated the situation. This fearsome disease added to the physical and mental suffering of the beleaguered population and increased the overall mortality.

Fever appears to have been a feature of the country for hundreds of years. Twelfth-century visitors commented on its extent and prevalence, while Gerald Boate, writing in the 1650s, called it 'malignant fever' and said it was 'commonly accompanied with a great pain in the head and in all the bones, great weakness, drought, loss of all manner of appetite, and want of sleep, and for the most part idleness or raving, and restlessness or tossings, but no very great nor constant heal'. In later centuries, fever was variously described as the country's 'scourge and chief destroyer', its 'great element of destruction' for hundreds of years. Eighteenth and nineteenth-century doctors did not know how the disease originated. Some contended that famine was the sole or paramount cause, others that food shortage was only one of several possible factors. Among these were poverty, the wretched housing of the poor, the paucity and inferior quality of their diet, their lack of clothing and fuel, dirt, depression, and intoxication, not to mention the pig in the kitchen and the middens that disgraced the frontage of every cabin in the country.

Some Irish medical practitioners traced the country's recurring outbreaks of fever to some unknown connection between atmospheric or electrical phenomena and the generation of disease, the so-called 'epidemic constitution'. This was entirely beyond the power of man to control or even comprehend properly. According to the distinguished Dublin physician and teacher, Robert J. Graves, the 'epidemic constitution' was some general atmospheric change that affected the whole island simultaneously. The definitions offered by his colleagues were equally vague. To one, it was an influence in the air, an unspecified 'something', to another the 'epidemic constitution' was 'some potent aerial poison'. One of the few specific explanations offered was that of a medical practitioner in King's County (Offaly) who attributed an outbreak of fever at Aghamon in November 1848 to an aurora borealis which, he claimed, had shone brilliantly over the entire district.

It is now known that the vector of fever was not famine, nor social distress, still less atmospheric abnormalities, but *pediculus humanus*, the human body louse. It is also known that there were two distinct but symptomatically related infections involved, typhus fever and relapsing fever. The typhus infection can enter the body through scratches on the skin, through the conjunctiva (the lining of the eye), or by inhalation, while relapsing fever is generally contracted through the skin. Typhus symptoms include high fever, prostration, mental confusion, body aches and a characteristic rash which covers the trunk and limbs of the body. In cases which are not going to recover, death usually occurs from heart failure about the fourteenth day. High temperature, generalised aches and pains, nausea, vomiting, nose bleeding and jaundice are features of relapsing fever. In cases with a favourable outcome, the fever ends after five or six days with a sharp crisis attended by profuse sweating and exhaustion. This drop in body temperature was colloquially known as 'getting the cool'. The symptoms return after about a week and there may be several such relapses before the disease runs its course.

During the Great Famine, relapsing fever was the prevalent disease among the general population, while the higher social classes tended to contract the more deadly typhus fever, especially those who were most exposed to infection, notably clergymen, doctors, members of relief committees and those connected with the administration of the poor law. The mortality rate from typhus was also more pronounced among the middle and upper classes than it was among the poor, who may have developed some immunity through long-term exposure.

The relationship between famine and fever is complex, but there is no direct nutritional connection. Increased vagrancy and mendicancy, as well as over-crowding and the neglect of personal and domestic hygiene, all of them features of famine, created the optimum social conditions for lice infestation. In Ireland in the late 1840s, infected lice feasted on the unwashed and susceptible skin of the hungry, multiplied in their filthy and tattered clothing, and went forth, carried the length and breadth of the country by a population who had taken to the roads, vagrants and beggars, as well as the evicted and those who had abandoned their homes voluntarily. Lice found new and unresisting hosts at food depots and relief works, at social and religious gatherings, and in many public institutions, such as prisons and workhouses.

Reports from various parts of the country suggest that the first stage of the prevailing 'famine fever' was relatively mild. An account from the island of Inishbofin, off County Galway, stated that the initial attack was so slight that the afflicted 'walked or rather staggered about with it', while a Dublin doctor related that many passed through the fever 'while they were literally walking about'. A characteristic of 'famine fever' was the voracious hunger displayed by the patient after the attack had ended. 'The hunger was in their hearts', said a nurse from Queen's County (Laois). When the relapse occurred, it was invariably more prolonged and severe. A County Limerick doctor reported that 'the relapsed stage was long, from ten to fourteen days, very severe, attended with great debility and prostration of strength'. These recurring bouts of fever further weakened an already debilitated population and left them very vulnerable to a host of other infections, notably dysentery and diarrhoea.

The term 'dysentery' was formerly applied to any condition in which inflammation of the colon was associated with the frequent passage of bloody stools. The term is now restricted to amoebic dysentery, which is almost entirely confined to tropical and sub-tropical countries, and to bacillary dysentery, an infectious disease which may occur sporadically or in epidemics. The disease is caused by the dysentery bacillus and the infection is spread by flies, by direct contact, or by pollution of the water by faeces infected with the bacillus. Symptoms vary from a mild attack of diarrhoea to an acute fulminating infection. The duration of the diarrhoea varies from a few days to a fortnight, depending upon the severity of the attack. There may also be nausea, aching pain in the limbs, and shivery feelings, while there is always fever. An attack cannot develop except through the agency of the specific bacillus. However, anything which causes an intestinal upset, such as unsuitable food, predisposes to infection. Dysentery is rendered more virulent by famine and by the concurrence of other exhausting diseases.

During the terrible winter of 1846-47, chronic dysentery, or 'starvation dysentery' as it was sometimes called, was reported to be very prevalent among the destitute. In west Cork, which was one of the worst famine affected areas of the country, one doctor noted that the pulse of those suffering from this horrible affliction was almost entirely absent, that the extremities of the body were livid and cold, the face haggard and ghost-like, the voice barely audible and reminiscent of the cholera whine. The smell from evacuations was very offensive, almost intolerable, he said, and was similar to that of 'putrid flesh in hot weather'. The discharges continued unabated until the body wasted to a skeleton. One Cork city doctor commented on the 'loathsome, putrid smell' that surrounded the diseased, as if, he said, 'the decomposition of the vital organs had anticipated death'.

Smallpox, which appeared epidemically in a very malignant form during the Great Famine, is no longer an active infection. It was an acute viral disease which was generally transmitted by airborne droplets. The characteristics of smallpox were high fever, headache, pain in the back and muscles, and occasionally in children vomiting and convulsions. In the severest infections, extreme toxaemia and massive haemorrhaging into the skin, lungs and other organs could cause death very quickly. In most cases, the afflicted survived to experience the characteristic rash two to five days after onset. Shortly afterwards, the small pimples of the rash turned to pustules, the drying and crusting of which began on the eighth or ninth day after the first eruptions. The scabs fell off three or four weeks after the commencement of the disease, leaving the victim invariably with a pocked and scarred face. Blindness was a possible consequence, as was infertility in males.

Infectious diseases, such as fever, dysentery and smallpox, terrified the poor, and with good reason. Such afflictions pauperised, when they did not kill, and reduced the most vulnerable and oppressed to squalid misery and despair. Fever had a devastating impact on the already precarious existence of the poor. Each attack, with the weakness it left behind, lasted about six weeks and, with successive family members being struck down, fever might persist in a poor man's cabin for months on end. Convalescence was slow and tedious, often taking six weeks and more, by which time a wage earner's family could be reduced to absolute poverty. Illness drove the poor into the pawn shops or compelled them to sell their meagre possessions, a pig, a cow, their miserable household furniture, or reduced them to the ultimate degradation, begging in public.

The fear of infection and the general acceptance of the contagiousness of fever and other epidemic diseases led to the establishment of special hospitals for the isolation of the infected. Three different types of institutions, county, district and poor law union fever hospitals, evolved during the first half of the nineteenth century. The poor law union fever hospitals were the most recent, dating from 1843. They were supported out of the rates and were open to all who resided within the poor law union. County fever hospitals, which admitted the infected from all parts of a given county, were entirely supported by local taxation. They evolved fitfully and by the time of the Famine not every county had one. District fever hospitals, which dated from the 1816-19 fever epidemic, were supported by a combination of local philanthropy and local rates. Unlike county fever hospitals, there was no limit to the number which could be established. However, their method of funding, not least the necessity of raising local subscriptions on an annual basis, retarded their development. At the commencement of the famine, there were about 100 permanent fever hospitals in the country.

Additional accommodation was provided for the infected in wooden sheds and tents, which were often pitched in the grounds of existing hospitals. In those parts of the country where there were no medical institutions of any description, the sick, when not abandoned to their own devices, were isolated as far as possible at home or quarantined in so-called 'fever huts'. These were wretched structures of mud or stone which were hastily thrown up at the side of a road, the corner of a field, or the verge of a bog. Some were even more rudimentary, consisting of nothing more than straw and furze tied together and placed at an angle to the ditch. In these primitive shelters, the hapless, isolated victims of fever struggled with cold and damp, hunger and thirst, as well as infection, totally dependent on the benevolence of others and the vagaries of fate.

Domestic quarantine, which was variously inspired by family affection, the absence of hospitals or the fear of entering them, was also a feature, one which was resorted to by rich and poor alike, although one pre-famine report from County Kilkenny suggests that it was the class of 'comfortable farmers' who were most likely to resort to the practice. In single-roomed dwellings, those afflicted with fever were placed at one end of the cabin, while the healthy attempted to ward off infection as best they could at the other. In more substantial dwellings, the practice was to isolate the sick in a room by blocking up the door with sods. A hole was made in the rear wall, through which the medical attendant had to scramble on all fours. Some doctors blamed the very high rate of mortality from fever among their colleagues on having to spend so much time in what one of them called 'the wretched cabins of the poor'. The popular attitude to fever hospitals was often ambiguous. There was a widespread suspicion that these institutions were sources of infection, a suspicion which hardened during the Great Famine when 373 emergency institutions were added to the 100 or so fever hospitals already in existence. The presence of a temporary fever hospital in a district, or the proposal to establish one, often provoked a very powerful response. For instance, an attempt by the famine relief committee in Clonakilty, County Cork, to open such an institution at the beginning of 1846 was thwarted by the general refusal to rent premises to them, either in or outside the town. It appears that the merest rumour of their intention to do so was sufficient to cause a panic wherever they went. Similarly, a poor law inspector reported from County Kerry in June 1847 that it was impossible to procure a house for use as a fever hospital in any small town in the Killarney union. 'The inhabitants positively refuse it through apprehension of fever', he said.

In December 1846, the board of health in Drumkeeran, County Leitrim, resolved to hire a house for use as a fever hospital, there being no such institution within a radius of eighteen miles. The proposal caused 'inconceivable alarm' in the town. Sixty-two of the residents, including merchants, shopkeepers, tradesmen, labourers, publicans, and householders, as well as Pat Gallaher, the schoolmaster, addressed a memorial to the Lord Lieutenant, objecting to the establishment of a fever hospital in the centre of the town. They stated that they were not so much opposed to the institution, as to its location. The layout of the town was such that fever patients would have to be transported through the main street, a necessity which they maintained posed an unacceptable risk to the town's 600 inhabitants and to visitors on market day and fair day. They were also concerned about the threat to the commerce and trade of the entire locality. The appellants urged the Lord Lieutenant to protect their families and themselves from what they termed 'an immediate exposure to plague' by directing that the proposed hospital be established outside the town.

A rather similar appeal was made by the residents of Kinvara, County Galway, in July 1847. They claimed that the imminent opening of a fever hospital in the town placed their lives and those of their families in 'the greatest peril'. They argued that the chosen site was too close to the town, that it either adjoined or was within eight feet of a range of houses occupied by some 300 individuals and was no more than sixty yards from the town centre. In the summer of 1847, the inhabitants of Killeshandra, County Cavan, threatened to pull down any fever shed that might be erected in the town, despite the fact that fever raged throughout the district. The temporary fever hospital at Fethard, County Tipperary, which had been opened in June 1847, was denounced from the altar on several occasions. The ambition of the parish priest and his curate, as they informed their flock repeatedly, was to see grass growing at the door of the hospital. One of their clerical harangues was delivered prior to the opening of a detached convalescence ward. Later that night, the building was maliciously burned to the ground. (A similar arson attack had occurred in Belturbet, County Cavan, in April 1847.)

Such extreme responses were prompted by fear of contagion, although, contrarily, the same fear prompted calls for the establishment of temporary fever hospitals, where the infected could be isolated. In all, 576 such applications were received by the Central Board of Health, the authorising body, between February 1847 and August 1850, when the board was finally dissolved. Three hundred and seventy-three of these were granted, the first at Tullamore, King's County, on 26 February 1847, followed by Mitchelstown, County Cork, on 3 March. The last temporary fever hospital was established at Lisnaskea, County Fermanagh, on 17 October 1849. The weekly hospital returns demanded by the board of health showed that 332,462 patients were treated in these institutions from July 1847 to the disbandment of the service three years later. More females than males were accommodated, 173,723 as opposed to 158,739, but male mortality was higher. A total of 34,622 individuals died in the temporary hospitals, a death rate of 10.4 per cent. Despite the hostility that was levelled at these institutions, they alleviated suffering and saved lives. Given the sheer scale of the famine, the failure of government to provide adequate financial support, and the relatively unadvanced state of contemporary medical practice, this was as much as could be expected of them.

Many doctors acknowledged their professional limitations and their inability to check the pestilence which raged around them. They were aware that dearth and disease were closely linked. They also knew that they did not have the antidote, that there was little they could do to counteract illness which originated in squalor and starvation. The political intervention they sought was overtaken by the natural. Famine-related death and emigration depleted the reservoir of disease in Ireland and the incidence of fever and other infectious diseases was significantly reduced in the wake of the disaster.

Chapter 11

'Lost children'? Irish famine orphans in Australia

Trevor McClaughlin

etween 1848 and 1850 over 4,000 young women between the ages of fourteen and twenty arrived in Sydney, Melbourne and Adelaide, some from Dublin, Belfast and Cork, others from famine-ravaged rural districts around Skibbereen, Ballina, Roscrea and Loughrea. Their emigration was the brainchild of Henry, earl Grey, Secretary of State for War and the Colonies, and was primarily designed to meet an Australian demand for domestic servants and marriageable young women. Grey's own Irish connections may also have prompted him to do something, however small, for an Ireland in the grip of famine.

Unlike the Irish who fled from the famine to North America, the death rate among orphan girls to Australia was very low—less than 1 per cent. Their emigration was closely regulated and watched over by government institutions such as the Irish Poor Law Commission in Dublin, the Colonial Land and Emigration Commission in London, and by immigration authorities in the Australian colonies. Behind it lay the experience of many years of convict transportation and bounty emigration, and these orphan girls arriving in the various Australian colonies often received an unfavourable reception. Such was the opposition to their immigration that Grey's scheme was short-lived. It came to a premature end scarcely two years after it began.

The orphan girls became caught up in a political contest between imperial and Australian interests; Australian money was being used to finance the immigration of Irish paupers. No doubt, also, the fact that the immigration scheme was perceived as Grey's, a secretary of state who was attempting to renew convict transportation, contributed to the hostile reaction to the orphans in Australia. But there was more involved than this. Other issues quickly came to the surface as well. Anti-Irish, anti-Catholic, and anti-female prejudice reared its head in a number of quarters. The young women were condemned in the colonial press, and by upper and middle-class opinion, as immoral, useless and untrained domestic servants, a drain upon the public purse, a financial liability, who, being blindly devoted to their religion, threatened to bring about a Popish ascendancy in New South Wales and Victoria. These were improper women, 'workhouse incapables' who were not carefully chosen migrants and were ill-suited to the needs of the Australian colonies. In the newspapers the orphans became the butt of prejudice and scorn. They were 'Irish orphans, workhouse sweepings' in the eyes of the *South Australian Register*; they were 'hordes of useless trollops, thrust upon an unwilling community', according to the *Melbourne Argus*. And in March 1850, the conservative *Sydney Morning Herald* complained that 'instead of a few hundreds, the girls are coming out by thousands. Instead of mere orphans, we are being inundated with Irish paupers'. The most strident criticism came from the *Melbourne Argus* in January 1850, which reflected the sectarian colour of local city politics:

> 'It is downright robbery to withhold our funds from decent eligible well brought up girls, to lavish it upon a set of ignorant creatures, whose knowledge of household duty barely reaches to distinguishing the inside from the outside of a potato, and whose chief employment hitherto has consisted of some intellectual occupation as occasionally trotting across a bog to fetch back a runaway pig. Our money ought to be expended upon the rosy cheeked girls of England, upon the braw (sic) lassies of bonnie Scotland, instead of being wasted upon these coarse, useless creatures who, with their squat, stunted figures, thick waists and clumsy ankles promises but badly for the 'physique' of the future colonists of Victoria.'

With opposition such as this the scheme was doomed. Imperial authorities soon gave way to colonial pressure and ceased sending Irish orphan girls to the Australian colonies.

So much for their immediate reception; but what became of them in the long-term, during their lives in Australia? We usually only come into contact with the 'subaltern' class in the past by means of intermediaries, such as officialdom. So too with the Irish orphan girls. We meet these young women most frequently at those points where the state intervened in their lives—in a workhouse in Ireland, on board a government chartered ship, in an immigration depot in Australia, at the drawing up or the cancellation of the indentures of domestic servants, and sometimes in the records of a police magistrate's court. These were the places where written records were set down. But state intervention was felt acutely for only part of these women's lives. The vast majority never appeared in a police magistrate's court. None kept a diary that has survived. There is no collection of their correspondence. How then are we to come close to these women and discover what became of them in the long run? How might their life stories be told?

Given the variety of backgrounds these young women came from, their relatively large number and the fact they were dispersed the length and breadth of eastern Australia, it is hardly surprising that their colonial experience should be equally varied. Among the casualties were those who were exploited and abused by their employers and husbands. In the Enniskillen workhouse register, for example, we find 'No 3708 Alice Ball, fourteen years old, orphan, Protestant, not disabled, Enniskillen town her place of residence, admitted 30 August 1848, discharged 3 October 1849'. She and her sister Jane made their way with other Enniskillen orphans to embark upon the *Diadem* at Plymouth for the voyage to Port Phillip Bay. Less than a year later, in April 1850, sixteen-year-old Alice, made pregnant by her employer, took her own life by throwing herself into Melbourne's River Yarra.

Mary Littlewood, also sixteen, endured harsh work conditions in Australia. Her mistress, Mrs Curtiss, of Sydney's North Shore, hammered her on the face until she was faint with loss of blood. Luckily a neighbour intervened on her behalf. Sent up the country to Scone, Mary again fell foul of her mistress, this time one Elinor McGrath, herself a recent arrival from Ireland. Something of Mary Littlewood's desperation, anger, frustration, rebellion, and even ano-mie (for how are we to describe it?) may be seen in the records relating to the cancellation of her indentures. Mary refused 'to obey' Mrs McGrath's 'lawful commands or attend to her duties as a servant'. Locked in, she attempted to burst the locks from the doors of her mistress's home, eventually 'tearing the curtains from the windows, seizing the sofa covers or tidies, and attempting to tear them to pieces, at the same time using the most blasphemous expressions against all around her, damning her soul to hell, but she would get out of the window and throw herself into the well'. Mary's indentures were cancelled and she was returned to the immigration depot at Maitland where she disappears from the record. Nothing further is known of her.

Seventeen-year-old Mary Colgan from Skibbereen arrived in Geelong in 1850 and had the misfortune to marry James Walton, a man 'addicted to liquor and using violence to his wife', as a judge was later to put it. At the Ballarat gold dig-gings in 1857 both were charged with the murder of Edward Howell. Mary got off, but James Walton was sentenced to eighteen months hard labour for manslaughter. A few years later, in 1862, still living in a tent, a long history of domestic violence came to a fatal climax. Mary, thrown into the cold night, beaten and kicked by her drunken husband, suffered a miscarriage. This was the fifth child she had lost because of her husband's beatings. A few days later she too died in the Ballarat District Hospital—'of typhoid fever and enteritis brought on by a miscarriage, occasioned by the ill-treatment of her husband'—according to the jury's verdict at her inquest. James Walton received seven years hard labour for his crime.

At the other end of the scale there were those who prospered, at least in the material sense. Ellen Parks, one of the Belfast girls who sailed in the infamous *Earl Grey*, was to marry London-born George Clarke, a successful restaurant keeper and oyster merchant in the city of Sydney. Like other Irish and Scottish women who suffered from deficiency diseases during the famine, Ellen had difficulties in childbirth in the early years. But she survived and eventually had nine children, six of whom were still alive at the time of Ellen's early death from heart disease in 1880. Ellen and George Clarke had prospered enough for Ellen to bequeath to her children not only money but jewellery, books, glassware, furniture and fine engravings—'a chester diamond ring to Ellen, a gold hunting watch with Albert and locket attached, to George, a gold miniature brooch, with Emu and Kangaroo in wreath, to Anna, a gold brooch and earrings containing topaz, to Alice'.

At Moreton Bay, in present day Queensland, Margaret Blair married a boot-maker, John Hardgrave, and together they accumulated extensive property holdings in both north and south Brisbane. When her husband died in 1908, Margaret inherited an estate valued at £9,450, a small fortune for those times. In Victoria, Letitia Connolly, like Alice Ball also from Fermanagh, married a storekeeper, Scottish born William Hayes. Grasping the opportunities that came their way in the fluid economic conditions of the gold-rush era, Letitia and William were to prosper in the Victorian country town of Dunolly. An enterprising merchant and investor, William left Letitia and their three children an estate valued at £7,487 when he died in 1890.

One of Letitia's shipmates, Sarah Richardson *née* Arbuckle, also married well. Married to a market gardener, farmer and landowner, she raised twelve children and died a 'gentlewoman' in 1908. After her husband died in 1892 Sarah managed the farm properties on Phillip Island herself. In the phonetic spelling of her entries in her meticulously kept farm account books we can still hear her Ulster accent. 'June 1899 for chicory digging, Petter Moor £4-12-6... August 10, 1900 paid to Hunary Richardson for work and laber don and bord-ing kiln men the sum of £18-1-0...in 1902 bard wire and chicory seed £1-3sh'.

Value of estate	<£100	£500	<£1000	>£10,000
Queensland	18% (3)	29% (5)	29% (5)	23% (4)
Victoria	6% (2)	69% (22)	c.13% (4)	c.13% (4)
N. S. W.	22% (8)	30% (11)	25% (9)	22% (8)
Total	15% (13)	45% (38)	21% (18)	20% (16)

From information in the author's prosopographical database of Irish female orphans, the orphans who went to Queensland fared marginally better than those in either New South Wales or Victoria. The table above is based on probate records.

Yet victimisation and abuse, or material prosperity and middle class resp-ectability was the lot of a minority of the famine orphans. In an attempt to find out what became of the majority of them, extensive research has been con-ducted among birth, death and marriage records in New South Wales, Victoria and Queensland. The demographic story of 280 young women has been pieced together using family reconstitution techniques.

Unfortunately, there are limitations to what this evidence uncovers. For example, our sample is biased towards Protestant Ulsterwomen. Nineteen per cent of the 1,285 orphans who disembarked at Port Phillip were Protestant and 28 per cent were born in the nine counties of Ulster. Of our reconstituted families, 37 per cent were Protestant and 43 per cent from Ulster. Our sample is also weighted towards the young women who arrived in the early vessels. The orphans became more difficult to trace as government assisted migrant traffic increased. Nonetheless, while acknowledging this bias, a very cautious alignment of names, ages, religion and parents' names (in the New South Wales and Queensland cases) carried through to immensely informative death certificates has led to a high degree of confidence in the accuracy of our findings.

Our typical famine orphan, if such a person ever existed, was a teenage servant from Munster who was Roman Catholic and able to read. Both her parents were dead (almost a quarter of those who came to New South Wales had one parent still alive). She married when she was nineteen, within two and a half years of disembarking in the colony (two thirds of those traced married in less than three years of their arrival) most likely to an Englishman, ten or eleven years her senior, and of a different religion from her own (30 per cent of those traced married Irishmen, 56 per cent Englishmen and 5 per cent native-born Australians). If she was lucky enough to survive the hazardous years of childbirth, her completed family size was nine children. The famine orphans had a higher age-specific marital fertility rate than other Irish born migrant women. In New South Wales and Victoria she could expect to live another forty years and in Queensland another fifty years after she arrived.

To try and put faces to some of our statistics, Mary Fitzgibbon from Clare was about eighteen years of age when she married Englishman John Hunter in Brisbane in 1853. He was twenty-five. Together they had nine children, four girls and five boys. John Hunter was a labourer, sawyer and timber cutter in Brisbane and on the Logan River. He died of rheumatic fever in 1873, one month before the birth of his youngest son, Peter. Mary was to live out another forty years of widowhood before being buried in Toowong cemetery. Honora Mugan from Castlebar in County Mayo married John Dengate, a Wesleyan, in Bathurst in 1852. She was eighteen, he almost twenty-seven. Together they had ten children, six boys and four girls. But they lost three of their boys in the scarlet fever epidemic in 1866. John died in Cooma in 1891. There is no record of Honora's death.

This is only some of the information that such records make available. They can be made to yield still more, about pre-marital pregnancy rates or about the orphans' geographic mobility, for example. The orphans were widely scattered in eastern Australia in 1861. Within fifteen years of their arrival, the famine orphans were concentrated in the major cities, but they were also in relative abundance on the frontiers of white settlement in New South Wales, Victoria and the newly created colony of Queensland.

Other inferences may be drawn from the demographic information contained in our family reconstitutions. The fact that the orphans married men who, on average, were ten or eleven years their senior, meant that many of them could look forward to prolonged widowhood. Margaret Best, for example, was twenty years a widow, Mary McCann fifty-three years, Jane Kirkwood forty-six, Ann Barrow fourteen and Honora Shea nearly twelve years without her husband. Because of this demographic fact, to say nothing of the effects of the economic depression of the 1890s and the absence, at this time, of an old age pension, a high proportion of Irish born working class widows would have been at great risk of institutionalisation in their old age. In 1848, Belfast orphan Mary Murray arrived in Adelaide on board the *Roman Emperor*. Forty-nine years later, in the 1890s, she was an inmate of a benevolent asylum at the other end of the country, at Dunwich on Stradbroke Island in Moreton Bay. So too were Ellen Leydon who had arrived by the *Thomas Arbuthnot*, and two other 'Belfast girls' who had come on the *Earl Grey*, Eliza Rodgers and Eliza Frazer.

Analysis of the occupational status of their husbands reveals that most of the famine orphans lived out a struggling, working class existence. Sarah Doyle's husband was a farm servant, police constable and fish dealer, Eliza Carrigge's a labourer and sawyer, Sarah McMullen's a labourer, milkman and dealer. Bridget Callery's was a labourer and bush carpenter, Ellen Dunbar's husband a boot and shoemaker, Bridie Flynn's a policeman and labourer, and Bridie McCarthy's a farm servant and labourer. They lived, in other words, in the kind of world so poignantly described in Australian literature in Henry Lawson's *The Drover's Wife*, in Barbara Baynton's *Bush Stories* and later, the novels of Ruth Park. Bearing children every two or three years and raising a large family in a two roomed wattle and daub hut was hardly more comfortable than life in the cramped living conditions of working class Sydney, Melbourne and Brisbane.

Materially well-to-do middle class matrons, victimised wives and servants, or battling working class mothers are the three dominant images of the famine orphans' lives in Australia. Yet even these representations are scarcely adequate; the orphans' life experience was as complex as the human condition itself. A young Scottish cuddy boy, James Porter, described the orphans who came to Moreton Bay at the end of 1849 being 'treated more like criminals than objects of pity. There (sic) hair had been cut short and the blackfellow when he saw them for the first time called them "short grass"; consequently they were afterwards called "short grasses"'. Porter's account is invaluable in evoking a picture of the rough masculine society into which the young women were thrown:

'The men from up country represented themselves or were understood by the girls to be squatters and when their cheques were spent the difficulty was to get their wives out of town...one girl refused to move but her husband by main force got her to the camp, padlocked a bullock chain about her waist and fastened it to the tail of the dray. Eighteen months afterwards I got on to the Merroo [gold] diggings. I recognised her living under the protection of a man other than her husband keeping a sly grog shop.'

We can only imagine how the young women came to terms with the rough masculine society of the day. Obviously some survived better than others. They should not be thought of simply as passive ciphers. They were self-fashioning women negotiating a space for themselves as best they could. Young orphan servants such as Mary Byrnes, Margaret Slack, Catherine Dempsey, Jane Sharp and Mary Moriarty used the law to defend their rights against their employers. In turn, employers complained of the sassiness and lack of deference on the part of their Irish orphan servants.

Similarly, the criteria we use to measure the 'success' of the famine orphans are difficult to define. For some of the orphans the very act of survival was success in itself. Others strove for middle class respectability and to suppress their workhouse origins. For many, one suspects the question of 'success' or 'failure' was not a consideration. For present day family historians increasingly interested in the Irish famine orphans, the best testimony to the young women's 'success' was their new Australian family. Ellen Maloney, for example, died of a uterine haemorrhage, scarcely forty years of age, but having given birth to ten children. Four generations later, numbered among a very large number of her descendants, are farmers, lawyers, academics, health professionals, public servants, men and women in religion, schoolteachers and business people. Eliza Frazer and Ellen Leydon may well have ended their days in Dunwich benevolent asylum. Very little, in fact, may be known of the emotional dynamics of their family life. But for their descendants, Ellen Leydon and Eliza Frazer are the founders of their own 'successful' Australian dynasties.

NB: Since the original publication of this essay in 2000 the author has continued to work on the topic; his findings can be read on his blog: https://earlgreysfamineorphans.wordpress.com

Chapter 12

Grosse Île: Canada's island famine memorial

Michael Quigley

T he approach to Grosse Île is dominated by the fifteen-metre-tall Celtic cross which bears the following inscription (in Irish):

'Children of the Gael died in their thousands on this island having fled from the laws of foreign tyrants and an artificial famine in the years 1847-48. God's blessing on them.'
'Let this monument be a token to their name and honour from the Gaels of America. God Save Ireland.'

It stands on a rocky promontory on Telegraph Hill, the highest point on the island. Built by the Ancient Order of Hibernians, it was unveiled on 15 August 1909 by the Papal Legate, Antonio Sbaretti, before a crowd of 9,000 people.

Grosse Île, isolated in the St Lawrence River but still close to Quebec City, opened as a quarantine station in 1832, in response to Canadian fears of that year's cholera epidemic in Europe spreading across the Atlantic. The failures of the quarantine station are measured in the burial sites of thousands of Irish immigrants, on the island and down the length of the St. Lawrence as far west as Hamilton. They died of cholera in 1832—and of typhus, ship fever and starvation while fleeing from the Great Hunger in the 1840s. At the western end of the island, between Cholera Bay and the Celtic cross on Telegraph Hill, is a long meadow, corrugated by a regular series of ridges, which inevitably remind the visitor of lazy beds, ridge-and-trench potato fields. On Grosse Île, too, the ridges are man-made, for they mark the mass graves where the Irish famine victims of 1847 were buried.

In February 1847, before the first ships arrived, Dr George Mellis Douglas, the medical superintendent, warned that the approaching season would bring 'a greater amount of sickness and mortality' and that the closure of American ports would 'augment the number of poor and destitute who will flock to our shores'. Douglas asked for £3,000 to expand the quarantine facilities to cope with the expected increase in numbers; he was given £300 to buy fifty extra beds.

In 1847 the shipping season in the St Lawrence opened as usual with the thaw in mid–May. The *Syria* was the first ship to arrive. She sailed from Liverpool on 24 March carrying 241 passengers and anchored at Grosse Île on 15 May. Six days later, 202 of the passengers from the *Syria* were ill. The quarantine hospital on the island, built for 150 patients, could barely accommodate 200, and was already filled to capacity.

Douglas was astonished by the 'unprecedented state of illness and distress' on the ships; he had 'never contemplated the possibility of every vessel arriving with fever as they do now', all of them carrying passengers 'in the most wretched state of disease'. On 23 May, he reported between fifty and sixty deaths per day. By the end of the month, 900 people had died and 1000 more fever cases were on the island, housed in hastily erected sheds and tents. Douglas was resigned to the prospect that many more would fall sick and require treatment. But since 'I have not a bed to lay them on or a place to put them in', he was obliged to flout the quarantine law and confine all passengers on board the ships at anchor in the river. By 31 May, forty ships lay off Grosse Île , with 12,500 passengers, old and young, healthy and sick, dying and dead, crammed into grossly overcrowded quarters, packed as human ballast in the holds of merchant vessels built to carry Canadian lumber to England.

Stephen de Vere from County Limerick, landlord, magistrate and social reformer, was no ordinary emigrant. He took passage on an emigrant ship to

41. *Landing at Grosse Île* by John Falter. (Courtesy of 3M Corporation)

provide a first-hand report to the Colonial Office. His account of conditions on the ship which, he was assured, was 'more comfortable than many', contained the following passage:

'Hundreds of poor people, men, women and children, of all ages from the drivelling idiot of ninety to the babe just born, huddled together, without light, without air, wallowing in filth, and breathing a fetid atmosphere, sick in body, dispirited in heart...the fevered patients lying between the sound in sleeping places so narrow, as almost to deny them a change of position... living without food or medicine except as administered by the hand of casual charity, dying without spiritual consolation and buried in the deep without the rites of the church.'

On 5 June 1847, when a Medical Commission appointed to examine the crisis on the island, there were 21,000 emigrants at Grosse Île. The death toll had tri-pled: 150 people were buried that day. The doctors found the sick on the island 'in the most deplorable condition, for want of the necessary nurses and hospital attendants'. On board the ships in the river, they reported 'corpses lying in the same beds with the sick and the dying'. They also noted the demoralisation of the victims, 'common sympathies being apparently annihilated by the mental and bodily depression produced by famine and disease':

'We entirely disapprove of the plan of keeping a vessel in quarantine for any period, however prolonged, whilst the sick and healthy are congregated together, breathing the same atmosphere, sleeping in the same berths, and exposed to the same exciting causes of contagion. This year's melancholy experience has in many instances proved that the number attacked and the mortality of the disease increased in direct ratio with the length of time the ship was detained under such circumstances. As an evidence of the truth of the above statement, we may be permitted to instance the case of the ship *Agnes* which arrived about sixteen days ago, with 427 passengers, out of which number not more than 150 are now in a healthy condition, the remainder being dead, or sick on board, or in hospital.'

Despite their criticism of Douglas's management of the quarantine station, they were unable to offer any remedy beyond instructing him to comply with the regulations—which was no longer possible. A month later, a special commit-tee of Quebec's Legislative Assembly examined witnesses to the disaster. They testified unanimously to the awful situation on the island. The sheds, tents and other buildings were overflowing. Beds, such as they were, were shared by as many as three people. Many fever victims were lying on bare planks or on the ground, the more fortunate on a bedding of straw.

42. The Famine monument on Telegraph Hill, Grosse Île. (Michael Quigley)

Fr Bernard McGauran, who led the first group of Catholic priests to the island, said, 'I have seen in one day thirty-seven lying on the beach, crawling in the mud and dying like fish out of water'. Fr William Moylan, parish priest of St Patrick's in Quebec City, told of seeing corpses left lying overnight in the bunks in the hospital 'even when they had a companion in the same bed'. He estimated the mortality as a result of confinement on the ships was 'at least twice as great as on shore' and said, 'the sick would have been better ashore under tents, having medical attendance close at hand, and besides would not have affected the healthy emigrants confined in the holds of the vessels with them'. On 20 July, when more than 2,500 fever cases were housed in the island hospitals, George Mountain, the Anglican Bishop of Montreal, described 'scenes of loathsomeness, suffering and horror, in the holds of the ships and in the receptacles for the patients'.

But even those who escaped confinement in the holds of the ships were not safe. De Vere said the hospital sheds on the island:

'Were very miserable, so slightly built as to exclude neither the heat nor the cold. No sufficient care was taken to remove the sick from the sound or to disinfect and clean the beddings. The very straw upon which they had lain was often allowed to become a bed for their successors and I have known many poor families prefer to burrow under heaps of stones, near the shore, rather than accept the shelter of the infected sheds.'

Fr Jean Baptiste Antoine Ferland reported that 'in the greater part of the sheds on Grosse Île , men, women and children are found huddled together in the same apartment...many who have entered the shed without any serious illness have died of typhus, which they have caught from their neighbours'.

In Ireland, the clearances of smallholders and 'cottiers' from the estates of major landlords added to the outflow of emigrants from Ireland. Major Denis Mahon of Strokestown, County Roscommon, while instructing his agent to evict more than 3,000 tenants, provided an exemplary summary of the landlords' economic motives: 'I think the first class for us to send is those of the poorest and worst description, who would be a charge on us for the poor house or for outdoor relief'. Eviction and the provision of 'assisted passage' was a cheaper option, and the arrival in Quebec of the first shipload of Mahon's evicted tenants struck Dr Douglas as noteworthy, due the horrific conditions that they had endured:

'The *Virginius* sailed from Liverpool, 28 May, with 476 passengers. Fever and dysentery cases came on board this vessel in Liverpool, and deaths occurred before leaving the Mersey. On mustering the passengers for inspection yesterday, it was found that 106 were ill of fever, including nine of the crew, and the large number of 158 had died on the passage, including the first and second officers and seven of the crew, and the master and steward dying, the few that were able to come on deck were ghastly yellow looking spectres, unshaven and hollow cheeked, and, without exception, the worst looking passengers I have ever seen; not more than six or eight were really healthy and able to exert themselves.'

As he was writing this report, two more ships commissioned by Mahon arrived. On the *Naomi*, Douglas said, 'the filth and dirt in this vessel's hold creates such an effluvium as to make it difficult to breathe'; 196 of her 421 passengers died before she reached Quebec. The *Erin's Queen* sailed with 493 people; 136 died at sea. On arrival at Grosse Île , the ship's master had to bribe his crew, at the rate of a sovereign per corpse, to remove the dead from the hold. Major Mahon himself was assassinated in Strokestown later that year.

As the summer wore on, the dying continued. 'Six men are constantly employed', said Douglas, 'digging large trenches from five to six feet deep, in which the dead are buried.' So many were interred, two or three deep, and so close to the surface, Douglas had to arrange to bring soil from the mainland to cover the dead. Even so, rats came ashore from the ships to feast on the cadavers.

In early July, Douglas finally addressed the critical problem of congregating the sick and healthy on board the ships. Attempting to prevent the spread of disease by segregating the healthy from the sick, he instituted a form of triage. He set up a tent camp at the eastern end of the island to shelter the healthy. The new hospital area was made permanent by the rapid construction of a dozen prefabricated wooden hospital sheds. By August, the hospital sheds and tents could accommodate some 2,000 sick people, 300 convalescents and as many as 3,500 healthy people. The year-end summary report of public works on the island listed a total of twenty-two hospital sheds.

Unfortunately, the primitive level of medical knowledge was compounded by the sheer size of the task. Despite good intentions, segregation was at best a palliative measure. At worst it exacerbated the situation, spreading the disease even more widely. Fr Bernard O'Reilly told the inquiry he had given the last rites to fifty people, on one July day, among the 'healthy' in the east-end tents; twenty-seven deaths among the healthy were recorded on July 31; and a month later the *Montreal Gazette* reported eighty-eight deaths in one week in the eastern zone. In September, as the shipping season drew to a close, there were still 14,000 people held in quarantine on board the ships at anchor off Grosse Île . Twelve hundred of the sick were transferred to the hospitals at the east end of the island on 13 September, to allow Douglas and his staff to fumigate the sheds and tents at the western end. As late as 16 September, the *Quebec Mercury* reported a large number of dysentery cases among the healthy. In the first three weeks of October, the parish register of St Luke's church on the island recorded ninety-seven anonymous burials. At the end of October, after the first snowfall of the winter, the final sixty patients on the island were transferred to hospitals at Quebec and Montreal and the Grosse Île quarantine station closed for the winter.

As early as 8 June, Douglas had warned the Canadians of the imminent danger of the spread of disease:

'Out of the 4,000 or 5,000 emigrants who have left this island since Sunday, at least 2,000 will fall sick somewhere before three weeks are over. They ought to have accommodation for 2,000 sick at least at Montreal and Quebec, as all the Cork and Liverpool passengers are half dead from starvation and want before embarking; and the least bowel complaint, which is sure to come with change of food, finishes them without a struggle. I never saw people so indifferent to life; they would continue in the same berth with the dead person until the seamen or captain dragged out the corpse with boat hooks. Good God! what evils will befall the cities wherever they alight. Hot weather will increase the evil. Now give the authorities of Quebec and Montreal fair warning from me. I have not time to write, or should feel it my duty to do so. Public safety requires it.'

Later that year, in a work entitled *The Ocean Plague*, Robert Whyte recalled his journey as a cabin passenger, sailing from Newry. He forecast more deaths, as his fellow passengers 'wandered over the country, carrying nothing with them but disease, and that but very few of them survived the severity of the succeeding winter, ruined as their constitutions were, I am quite confident'. While nothing is known of Whyte beyond this account, his suggestion that many of the new Irish arrivals were doomed was echoed in the observations of other contemporaries. 'Those who are healthy, if sent up as hitherto to Montreal, must bring with them the seeds of sickness', said Fr O'Reilly, 'while out of the numbers who can leave Montreal for a further destination, the large majority are pre-doomed to expire on the wharves of Kingston or Toronto, and to carry with them whithersoever they direct their steps, the dreadful malady that now hangs over the country like a funeral pall'.

These gloomy predictions were all too accurate. In Montreal, the growing danger of contagion—the death toll reached thirty people a day in June—led to the establishment of a second quarantine station. Hospital sheds and open-sided shelters for the healthy were built at Point St Charles, forming 'a large square with a court in the centre where the coffins were piled, some empty waiting for the dead, some full awaiting burial'. Twelve years later, when the site of the fever sheds and mass graves was cleared for construction of the Victoria Bridge, the workers—mostly Irish—downed tools and refused to continue until a proper memorial was built. They dredged a huge black stone out of the river and had carved on it the inscription 'to preserve from desecration the remains of 6,000 immigrants who died from ship fever AD 1847-48 this stone is erected by the workmen of Messrs. Peto, Brassey and Betts employed in the construction of the Victoria Bridge AD 1859'.

The Montreal experience was repeated as the epidemic swept down the St Lawrence from Quebec to the western end of Lake Ontario. The emaciated, starving, destitute and febrile Irish brought disease and misery with them. They caused alarm and fear but, for the most part, charity outweighed xenophobia in the Canadian response. Indeed, the story of 1847 is as much one of Canadian generosity as it is of Irish suffering. Fever sheds were built, the victims were hastily segregated, and they were tended—tirelessly and heroically—by clergy and laity in each community, but still they died in their thousands.

And as the Irish died, they infected their hosts. At Grosse Île, two of the seventeen Anglican clergymen died, as did four of the forty-two Catholic priests who served there. Douglas also reported the deaths of thirty-four workers: stewards, nurses, orderlies, cooks, policemen, and carters. The 'ocean plague' exacted its price further afield, claiming more victims in Quebec City, Montreal, Kingston and Toronto. Among the nurses of the Order of Grey Nuns, most fell ill and several died. Nine priests including Fr Hudon, Vicar-General of Montreal, died in that city. In November, John Mills, the mayor of Montreal whose energy and altruism ensured relatively safe and healthy conditions for the famine victims, caught the fever at the sheds and died. The same fate befell Toronto's first Catholic bishop, Michael Power. Like other witnesses, Bishop Mountain of Montreal was particularly touched by the plight of the hundreds of children orphaned by the epidemic. Among the dozens of miserable waifs, a couple particularly caught his attention: a dying child, huddled under a pile of rags in one of the tents; and the body of a little boy who was walking with his friends, sat down to rest under a tree, and died.

The most resonant part of the story is the fate of the 2,000 children orphaned at Grosse Île . Fr Charles-Félix Cazeau, 'priest to the Irish' and future Vicar-General of Quebec, oversaw the childrens' future. In Quebec and Montreal, Catholic charities took charge of the children and the priests went on the circuit of parishes in Quebec urging the faithful to adopt them. Fr Thomas Cooke of Trois Rivieres wrote that his parishioners were arguing over the right to adopt the orphans. That so many Irish names continue to exist in Quebec, in the francophone population, testifies to astonishing magnanimity, for many of the adopted children were allowed to retain their Irish names.

At the end of the year, Douglas raised a monument at the mass graveyard on Grosse Île , to mark the sacrifice of the four doctors—Benson, Pinet, Malhiot and Jameson—who 'died of typhus fever contracted in the faithful discharge of their duty upon the sick'. Dr John Benson is a striking symbol of the whole complex of the epidemic of 1847. He was a sixty-year-old physician with experience in the fever hospitals in Ireland, who had been evicted from an estate in Castlecomer, County Kilkenny. He arrived at Grosse Île on the *Wandsworth* on 20 May, volunteered to assist Dr Douglas, contracted typhus and died within a week. The monument also bears this inscription: 'In this secluded spot lie the mortal remains of 5,424 persons who, fleeing from pestilence and famine in Ireland in the year 1847, found in America but a grave'.

On St Patrick's Day 1996, Sheila Copps, Deputy Prime Minister and Minister of Canadian Heritage, announced plans for a National Historic Site at Grosse Île, a designation it now possesses. The minister's announcement was the culmination and vindication of a four-year-long campaign to prevent the Parks Service from turning it into a Canadian Ellis Island. In the longer view, it marked a full century of activity by Irish Canadians to assert the importance of Grosse Île, from the commemoration of the fiftieth anniversary of the Great Hunger in 1897 to Irish President Mary Robinson's visit in 1994. Fittingly, since 1998 it has been twinned with Strokestown Park Famine Museum, linking both the origin point and destination of many of those who migrated from Ireland to Canada during the Great Famine.

Chapter 13

The vanishing Irish: Ireland's population from the Great Famine to the Great War

Timothy W. Guinnane

Many countries today face, or will soon face, one of two population problems. Some countries' populations are growing so rapidly that sheer numbers will endanger their ability to provide schooling, employment, and basic social amenities to their people. Other countries face a situation nearly the opposite. Their population growth is very slow, or in some cases, numbers are declining. Ireland faced *both* of these problems during the nineteenth century: in the decades prior to the Great Famine of the 1840s, Ireland's population grew at then-unprecedented rates, while for over a century after, the population shrank continuously. By 1911 there were in Ireland about half as many people as in 1841. Less than half of the total depopulation can be attributed to the famine itself. The rest reflects low birth-rates and high emigration rates.

Depopulation was not confined to Ireland in the late nineteenth century. Agricultural transformation at home and the pull of higher wages in cities and abroad reduced the rural population in several regions of Britain and other European countries. Ireland's depopulation caused considerable comment, as observers saw in the loss of people the loss of national vitality, a perspective often underpinned by the assumption that there was something unique about Ireland's population history, including the depopulation. This assumption has been challenged by Ireland's economic and demographic historians. Using new sources and methods, and by comparing Ireland carefully to other, similar European countries and regions, historians have come to view this depopulation as fascinating and unusual, but reflecting quite general forces at work across Europe at the time.

Depopulation in Ireland was primarily a rural affair, as it was elsewhere in Europe. Ireland's depopulation reflects a demographic regime that combined three elements, each of which was unusual but not unique in western Europe at the time: the decline of marriage, the creation of large families by those who did marry, and heavy emigration. Post-famine Irish marriage patterns were an extreme example of a long European tradition. For centuries young people in western Europe had delayed their marriages more than elsewhere, with women rarely marrying before their early twenties, and in most populations some 10 to 20 per cent of adults never married at all. (Demographers call never-married adults 'celibates', but the term does not necessarily imply sexual chastity. Religious celibates were only a small portion of never-married adults in Europe—Ireland included.) Marriage in post-famine Ireland declined in popularity to the point where, in 1911, about one-quarter of all adults in their forties had never married. A second feature of Ireland's distinctive demographic conditions reflected not change in itself, but rather a pace of change that was,

43. Overpopulation in the nineteenth century, Gweedore, County Donegal. (National Library of Ireland)

relative to other European countries, very slow. Elsewhere in western Europe in the late nineteenth century, couples began the widespread adoption of contraception. By 1900, couples in countries like England or Germany were having only half as many children as those in their parents' generation. Ireland's fertility decline was by comparison late, and many Irish couples continued to have large families long after this practice was uncommon elsewhere in western Europe. (Another common element of demographic systems elsewhere, children borne to unwed mothers, was comparatively rare in Ireland.) Finally, emigration from Ireland increased during the famine and remained extensive afterwards. The rate of emigration from Ireland was often higher than for any other European country during the second half of the nineteenth century. In sum, the fewer and fewer marriages in Ireland did not produce enough children to offset the numbers who chose to spend their lives overseas, resulting in an ever–smaller Irish population.

These trends sound exotic today, and by the standards of some of western Europe at the time they were odd indeed. But no individual element of this system was unique to the Irish. Ireland might have had more bachelors and spinsters than any other European country in 1900, but several countries were close behind, and in several European regions marriage was nearly as unpopular as it had become in Ireland. Ireland's fertility transition was relatively late and half-hearted by the standards of England or Germany, but once again Ireland had company in its high fertility levels early in the twentieth century. Emigration was not restricted to Ireland, either. Millions left Germany during the middle of the nineteenth century, and later on Scandinavia and southern and eastern Europe experienced mass emigration.

Yet Ireland's depopulation remains interesting even if not unique. First and most importantly, the decline of Irish population from over eight million to

44. This 1860s photograph of a sod cabin exemplifies the extreme poverty of rural Ireland. (George Morrison Collection)

just over four million made for a very different country. Second, even if Ireland shared a particular population pattern with, say, Scotland, we still want to know why this trend emerged in Ireland. Finally, the *combination* of marriage, fertility, and emigration that characterised post-famine Ireland *was* unique, or nearly so; other places had elements of the Irish demographic regime, but only the Irish combined those elements in just this way. Why Ireland's depopulation took this form tells us much about Irish society and the rural economy in the period between the Great Famine and the Great War.

Ireland's marriage patterns have invited considerable comment but less systematic research. Two kinds of explanations enjoy some currency among scholars. The first argues that marriage declined in the decades after the famine because people felt their incomes were less and less able to support the expense of marriage and children. This Malthusian interpretation owes much to the pioneering research of Kenneth H. Connell, who argued that Irish farming families became increasingly unwilling to subdivide their farms or to provide dowries for more than one daughter, leaving many of their children to choose between emigration and a life of permanent celibacy in Ireland. There is a basic problem with this reasoning: average incomes in Ireland increased considerably in the decades after the famine, until by 1914 the average rural person was much better off than his grandparents had ever dreamed of. According to the

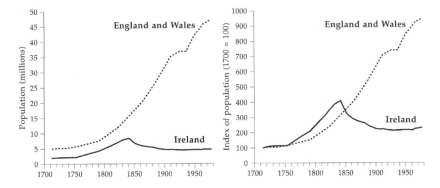

45. The left-hand graph shows absolute population sizes in millions. The right-hand graph uses index numbers (1700=100) to compare the growth of the two. Sources: Ireland for pre-1821 data are Clarkson's estimates as reported in Mokyr and Ó Gráda 1984, table 1; for 1821 and later, estimates are from the official census, as reported in Vaughan and Fitzpatrick 1978, table 3; England and Wales, pre-1821 data are estimates by Wrigley and Schofield 1981, table A3.1; for 1821 and later, estimates are from the official census as reported in Mitchell 1980, series b1.

Malthusian logic, this increase in incomes should have produced an *increase* in marriage rates.

A second style of explanation stresses a combination of cultural and psychological barriers to marriage. There are many styles to this explanation, and some doubtless contain a germ of truth. One version says that dutiful sons and daughters who delayed their own marriages to care for aged parents might have found themselves too old to make a comfortable marriage once their own filial obligations were past. This is a central theme in literary works such as Patrick Kavanagh's 1942 poem *The Great Hunger*, where the farmer's son Maguire remains 'faithful' to his mother until he is sixty-five years old. However fair as a characterisation of some individual cases, this kind of explanation begs the question of why such decisions were made more by Irish than by English people, and why they became more common in the late nineteenth century. Others have claimed that the Catholic Church discouraged marriage through various overt and subtle means. This claim is harder to credit. The Catholic Church *encourages* lay marriage, and the one-quarter of Irish people who were Protestant had very similar marriage patterns. In any case, Irish historians have usually stressed the Catholic Church's role in providing solace for those left alone because of Irish marriage patterns, rather than seeing the Catholic Church as a cause of those marriage patterns. Another style of psychological explanation of Irish marriage patterns claims to find in Irish families and culture a pathological attitude towards sex and sexual intimacy, leading to a fear of the opposite sex and of marriage. These arguments are not just insulting to Irish people, they overlook important historical facts: every bachelor or spinster in Ireland had a counterpart in other European countries, both in the nineteenth century and earlier, and a great number of counterparts in the other peasant regions of Europe. If Irish people were emotionally diseased, they had a great deal of company elsewhere. More importantly, we are trying to explain a *change* in marriage patterns, and nobody has put for a convincing story about changes in filial piety or sexual repression.

So why did so many Irish people live out their days without marrying? My own view starts by looking more closely at those who did not marry. Emigration's effects show up in many subtle ways in Irish history, and they play an unappreciated role in this context. People who lived out their days without marrying in Ireland had chosen not only to remain single, but to remain in Ireland. In fact, Ireland's bachelors and spinsters in 1911 were a small minority of the total cohort into which they were born. To understand why Ireland had so many bachelors and spinsters, we have to explain not just why many Irish people decided not to marry, but why so many people remained in rural Ireland even knowing they were unlikely ever to marry there. (If we believe Malthusian accounts, that is, we are left wondering why a man who felt too poor to marry and to raise a family in Ireland did not simply join his compatriots in the richer economies abroad.) Remaining in rural Ireland, even as a permanent bachelor or spinster, held both economic and non-economic attractions missing in earlier accounts. Letters and other accounts of emigrant life often stress the harshness and insecurity of life in an industrial city abroad, in contrast to the comforts of familiar life and kinship networks for those who remained. Just having land, even if it meant remaining alone, was a source of security in uncertain economic times.

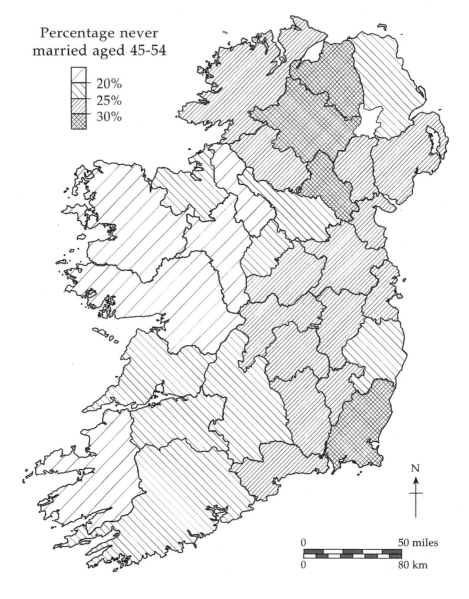

Percentage never
married aged 45-54

20%
25%
30%

N

0   50 miles
0   80 km

46. 1911 census, as abstracted in Vaughan and Fitzpatrick 1978, table 33.

The decline in marriage also reflects changes in what it meant for young people to marry. Rural marriages by all accounts were primarily partnerships to raise children and to run households, instead of the sources of emotional intimacy we think of today. Changes in the rural economy in the post-famine decades made it easier for country people to run their farms and to provide for their comforts in old age without marrying or having their own children. People became not poorer, as the Malthusian view would suggest, or afraid of the opposite sex, as psychological theories imply, but simply less willing to accept the burdens of marriage and a family because it was less important to satisfying the economic goals marriage had once served. Thus emigration became a less attractive alternative for those unlikely to marry in Ireland, and marriage became a less attractive alternative for those unwilling to emigrate. Put somewhat differently, most people who remained in Ireland probably *did* want to marry, under the right circumstances, but their notions of 'the right circumstances' became more narrowly defined, and they were increasingly willing to risk a situation—such as the fictional Maguire's, who could not marry while his mother was alive—that would prevent them from marrying at all.

Ireland's late fertility decline has always had an obvious explanation—the Catholic Church's opposition to contraception. This argument once again overlooks the behaviour of Ireland's Protestants. Careful comparison of the fertility of Catholic and Protestant couples in the early twentieth century has shown that while Catholic families were larger than Protestant, they were not *much* larger. In other words, even Ireland's Protestants were, by European standards, reluctant to use contraception. (And to make a different comparison, in some other Catholic regions of Europe family sizes declined long before they did in Ireland.) Whatever the role of moral and cultural opposition to contraception among both Catholic and Protestant Irish people, it is worth noting that the *economic* forces encouraging smaller families elsewhere in Europe were not at work to the same degree in Ireland. Elsewhere, the increasing participation of women in the paid labour force encouraged smaller families. In Ireland paid work opportunities for rural women actually declined in the late nineteenth century. And elsewhere in Europe concerns over the cost of educating and establishing children led parents to have fewer of them. For Irish parents, especially those in poor rural areas, setting up a child cost little more than a ticket to America or Australia.

Historians have often pointed to the emotional cost and sense of cultural dislocation experienced by Ireland's emigrants, but few have doubted that the vast majority left Ireland looking for better incomes elsewhere. Recently scholars have come to appreciate just how keenly young people in Ireland monitored the character of economic life abroad. Ireland's post-famine young people were, compared to other Europeans, unusually willing to pick up and leave home. Among major countries of emigration to the United States for example, a given difference between Irish and US wages would bring forth proportionally many more Irish emigrants than people from any other European country. Ireland had become a country where any improvement abroad or any economic crisis at home would quickly lead to a haemorrhage of her people.

Why were Irish demographic adjustments so unlike the adjustments underway in the major industrial countries of Europe? Some aspects of Irish demographic adjustment reflect historical facts that pre-date the famine, and in some cases predate the nineteenth century. One was the nature of land-holding. Irish historians long stressed supposed defects in Ireland's tenurial system as a reason for Irish poverty. The more important feature of Irish land tenure for demographic purposes was not the existence of landlords or the lack of leases, but the fact that most agriculturists in Ireland were peasants or relatively small farmers. The prevalence of these people among Ireland's agrarian classes was only strengthened by the famine and subsequent developments, as the cottiers and labourers who had been so important prior to the famine virtually disappeared from the countryside. This is very different from England's agrarian structure, where most agriculturists were landless labourers working for farmer-entrepreneurs. For those holding land or related to those holding land, virtually every demographic decision in Ireland reflected ties to land. Leaving Ireland meant settling claims to land, or cashing in one's potential claim to the land. Marrying meant acquiring land, by inheritance or dowry.

A second historical factor that led to Ireland's distinctive demographic adjustment was the Great Famine itself. By driving so many from Ireland in a short time, the famine solidified an already-strong emigrant tradition. Young people growing up after the famine could easily leave to join friends or relatives overseas. Thriving overseas Irish communities could finance emigration to a degree otherwise impossible in such a poor society. Once started, this emigration process meant that Ireland would remain a country of emigrants, as it has, and that virtually any economic crisis would lead to a heightened outflow. And that emigration would have profound effects on marriage and fertility, as we have already noted.

Is there no room in this view of post-famine demographic adjustment for a distinctive Irish culture? My focus on economic change and on the institutions of land-holding and rural households does take the focus off some supposedly unique Hibernian attitudes and customs. This is only right; Ireland was not the only European country to have large numbers of bachelors and spinsters, or for that matter strong mother-son bonds, strong religious traditions, or any of the myriad other proposed explanations for Irish demographic patterns. But neither does clarifying the role of economic change necessarily leave us with a nineteenth-century Irish society identical to all others. Looking back at demographic change in the decades after the famine suggests a more complicated process in which rural people adapted their behaviour in the face of economic pressures, and the new demographic patterns led to changes in attitudes that informed larger cultural changes. For example, children who grow up in a society where there are many single adults will think nothing ill of bachelors and spinsters, and perhaps be more likely to remain unmarried themselves. The demographic changes that swept Ireland between the Great Famine and the Great War reflected economic changes and specifically Irish responses to those changes. The result, over time, was a change in behaviour and attitudes that left lasting marks on Irish society.

Chapter 14

The Great Famine: Its interpreters, old and new

James S. Donnelly, Jr.

For many years now 'revisionist' Irish historians have delighted in debunking nationalist interpretations of the Irish past. In general revisionism has had a triumphal march, slaying one dragon of Irish nationalist historiography after another. In 1989 the revisionist enterprise received a serious challenge from the historian Brendan Bradshaw, who took the revisionist school to task for its pursuit of a kind of scientific, objective, value-free examination of the Irish past. Without subscribing fully to his arguments, I believe that he is essentially correct in asserting that numerous revisionist historians have not honestly and squarely confronted what he calls 'the catastrophic dimensions of the Irish past'. I wish to examine this question with reference to the Great Famine, focusing especially on the issue of the extent to which the British Government was responsible for mass death and mass emigration because of the policies which it did or did not pursue.

For revisionist historians the publication in 1962 of *The Great Hunger: Ireland 1845-1849* by Cecil Woodham-Smith was not an altogether welcome event. Perhaps they envied the book's commercial success: *The Great Hunger* was immediately a best seller on two continents, and its premier status as the most widely read Irish history book of all time has only grown with the years. But far more troubling to the revisionists was the 'ungoverned passion' to which numerous reviewers of the book succumbed. Vigorously protesting against this 'torrent of muddled thinking', the late F.S.L. Lyons, reviewing his work, called attention to a striking aspect of the popular response:

'Ugly words were used in many reviews — "race-murder" and "genocide," for example — to describe the British Government's attitude to the Irish peasantry at the time of the famine, and Sir Charles Trevelyan's handling of the situation was compared by some excited writers to Hitler's 'final solution' for the Jewish problem. This response to Mr Woodham-Smith's work was not confined to Irish reviewers, nor even to imaginative authors like Mr Frank O'Connor, but cropped up repeatedly in English periodicals also, occasionally in articles by reputable historians.'

THE FAMINE IN IRELAND.—FUNERAL AT SKIBBEREEN.—FROM A SKETCH BY MR. H. SMITH, CORK.—(SEE NEXT PAGE.)

47. Famine funeral at Skibbereen (*Illustrated London News*).

Among such reputable scholars Lyons must have had in mind A.J.P. Taylor, the distinguished, if controversial, historian of modern Germany, whose review of *The Great Hunger* appeared in the *New Statesman* and was later reprinted under the title 'Genocide' in his *Essays in English History*. At times Taylor sounded just like the famous Irish revolutionary nationalist John Mitchel. In the late 1840s, declared Taylor with a sweeping reference to the notorious German extermination camp, 'all Ireland was a Belsen'. He minced no words: 'The English governing class ran true to form. They had killed two million Irish people.' And that the death toll was not higher, Taylor savagely remarked, 'was not for want of trying'. As evidence, he offered the recollection of Benjamin Jowett, the Master of Balliol: 'I have always felt a certain horror of political economists since I heard one of them say that the famine in Ireland would not kill more than a million people, and that would scarcely be enough to do much good'.

Woodham-Smith himself was reasonably restrained in his conclusions, and Lyons absolved him of responsibility for what he saw as the emotionalism and the wholly inappropriate comparisons of the reviewers. But at the same time, he accused her of other serious faults: vilifying Charles Trevelyan, the key administrator of famine relief, and exaggerating his importance, failing to place the economic doctrine of *laissez-faire* firmly in its contemporary context and glibly using it as an explanatory device without acknowledging the looseness of this body of ideas, and in general committing the cardinal sin of the populariser — choosing narrative and description over analysis. Admittedly, his merits as a populariser were great. 'No one else', conceded Lyons, 'has conveyed so hauntingly the horrors of starvation and disease, of eviction, of the emigrant ships,

48. Charles Trevelyan

of arrival in Canada or the United States, of the terrible slums on both sides of the Atlantic to which the survivors so often found themselves condemned'. And if all that students wanted to know was 'what happened in the starving time and how it happened', then *The Great Hunger* would supply the answers. But they would have to turn elsewhere if they wanted 'to know the reasons why' — a rather unkind ironic wordplay with the title of Woodham-Smith's famous book about the British role in the Crimean War. Apparently, Lyons's stinging

49. Clothes being distributed at Kilrush, Co. Clare (*Illustrated London News*).

criticisms of Woodham-Smith were widely shared by other members of the Dublin historical establishment. In University College Dublin in 1963 history students encountered as the essay topic of a final exam the dismissive proposition, '*The Great Hunger* is a great novel'.

In saying that students of the famine who wanted to know the reason why would have to turn elsewhere, Lyons had in mind the academically acclaimed but much less famous 1957 book *The Great Famine: Studies in Irish History 1845-52*, edited by R. Dudley Edwards and T. Desmond Williams, two of the founding fathers of modern Irish historiography. The editors and contributors could not be accused of emotionalism or of politicising their tragic subject. They appear to have been quite anxious to avoid re-igniting old controversies or giving any countenance to the traditional nationalist-populist view of the Famine. The overall tone was set in the 'foreword', where Kevin B. Nowlan soothingly observed:

'In folklore and political writings, the failure of the British Government to act in a generous manner is quite understandably seen in a sinister light, but the private papers and the labours of genuinely good men tell an additional story. There was no conspiracy to destroy the Irish nation. The scale of the actual outlay to meet the Famine and the expansion in the public-relief system are in themselves impressive evidence that the state was by no means always indifferent to Irish needs. But the way in which Irish social problems so frequently overshadowed all else in the correspondence of statesmen testifies in a still more striking manner to the extent to which the British Government was preoccupied with the famine and distress in Ireland.'

The worst sins attributed by Nowlan to the British Government were its 'excessive tenderness' for the rights of private property, its 'different [and limited] view of its positive responsibilities to the community', and its inevitable habit of acting 'in conformity with the conventions of [the larger] society'. High politicians and administrators were not to be blamed; they were in fact innocent of any 'great and deliberately imposed evil'. Instead, insisted Nowlan, 'the really great evil lay in the totality of that social order which made such a famine possible and which could tolerate, to the extent it did, the sufferings and hardship caused by the failure of the potato crop'. In other words, no one was really to blame because everyone was.

Nowlan's complete lack of asperity was repeated by Thomas P. O'Neill in his pivotal chapter on the administration of relief. Although O'Neill was not uncritical of British policies or their implementation, his language was at times egregiously soft and his judgement lacking in firmness. Thus we are told that public relief officials 'throughout the country' were 'seriously overworked' but nonetheless 'gallantly endeavoured to bring the best possible result from the schemes laid down for them by the government'. The question is, the best possible result for whom? Certainly, often not for the famished and the diseased. Trevelyan too 'worked unceasingly', as if zeal can only be virtuous, and his plans had what are merely called 'faults', one of which was to insist that the cost of famine relief must always be a local charge. If instead, concluded O'Neill rather weakly, the British state had admitted that in the event of such a catastrophe its paramount responsibility was to save life, 'the Irish famine *might have been* more capably countered' (my italics).

Such charitable judgements about British relief policies and about the attitudes and motivations that lay behind them would presumably have been less easy to make if the editors had not decided to exclude from their volume a chapter by Brian Osborne on English public opinion, which exhibited deep hostility for the Catholic Irish in the wake of the 1848 rebellion, and which long before then often betrayed vehement racialist prejudices. But even in a chapter where issues relating to British responsibility might have been discussed in some detail, namely, that by Roger McHugh on the oral tradition which brings the volume to a close, there is a truly remarkable avoidance of engagement. It is not that McHugh, whose contribution to the volume is among the best, fails to mention how famine sufferers condemned this or that aspect of the administration of relief. But he never seriously examines the politicisation of the famine in Irish popular consciousness.

That their collective volume essentially failed to answer the basic question of British responsibility was recognised by at least one of the editors at the time. Soon after the book was published at the end of 1956, Dudley Edwards confided to his diary: 'If it is [called] studies in the history of the Famine, it is because they [the contributors?] are not sure all questions are answered. There are still the fundamental matters whether its occurrence was not due to the failure of the sophisticated to be alert'. By 'the sophisticated' I assume he means the political élite in Britain. Indeed, Edwards was aware much earlier, in 1952, that a merely mechanical yoking together of a series of specialist contributions on such subjects as politics, relief, agriculture, emigration, and folklore would 'fail to convey the unity of what was clearly a cataclysm in the Butterfield sense'. The need to comprehend and to portray the disaster as a whole was, he felt, inescapable. If this were done, it would 'also answer the question of responsibility, so unhesitatingly laid at England's door by John Mitchel'. But in the end, when the book was published, no comprehensive narrative was provided, and as a result, the powerful Mitchel indictment was not answered. Indeed, the book in which Mitchel most fully developed his indictment — *The last conquest of Ireland (perhaps)* originally serialised in 1856 — does not even appear in the bibliography.

One reason why Mitchel repels modern revisionist historians is that his language is so vehement in tone and so extreme in the substance of its accusations. His fullest statement that British policies amounted to genocide came near the end of his book, where he asserted that:

'[a] million and a half of men, women, and children were carefully, prudently, and peacefully *slain* by the English Government. They died of hunger in the midst of abundance, which their own hands created; and it is quite immaterial to distinguish those who perished in the agonies of famine itself from those who died of typhus fever, which in Ireland is always caused by famine...The Almighty indeed sent the potato blight, but the English created the famine.'

What exactly was it that convinced Mitchel, and by what evidence did he seek to convince others, that British policies were genocidal in both intent and result? First, there was the government's 'strict adherence to the principles of "political economy"' in spite of, or indeed because of, its consequences: the export of huge quantities of grain and livestock to Britain in the midst of famine; the refusal to sell relief supplies at less than market prices; and the wasteful expenditure of large sums on 'unproductive' public works. Mitchel was especially incensed by the government's refusal to close the ports to the outward shipment of grain and livestock, and he skilfully exploited the issue.

In fact, he badly misinterpreted what was really happening in the critical area of food supply. Irish grain exports decreased substantially during the Famine years, and imports, after a fatal delay, eventually soared. Even so, modern historians cannot reject the Mitchel perspective entirely. The stoppage of exports after the disastrous harvest of 1846, and before the arrival of large supplies of foreign grain early in 1847, might well have greatly slowed the onset of mass starvation and disease by providing a bridge between extreme food scarcity and relative abundance.

The force of Mitchel's case against the British Government, however, was (and remains) much stronger when he turned to consider the cost and character of those relief measures that he branded as 'contrivances for slaughter'. Repeatedly, he condemned the utter inadequacy of the British Government's financial contribution and the gross unfairness in a supposedly 'United Kingdom' of throwing almost the entire fiscal burden (after mid-1847) on Ireland alone. He portrayed in the darkest colours the economic results of the application (in the Poor Law Amendment Act of 1847) of the Whig maxim that Irish property must support Irish poverty. When the Irish poor law system teetered on the brink of collapse in 1849, prompting the Whig Government to bring forward a special scheme to aid bankrupt western unions (the Rate-in-Aid Act), the burden of furnishing relief was still confined exclusively to Ireland. 'Assuming that Ireland and England are two integral parts of a "United Kingdom" (as we are assured they are)', Mitchel declared almost gleefully, 'it seems hard to understand why a district in Leinster should be rated to relieve a pauper territory in Mayo, and a district in Yorkshire not'.

Mitchel detected the genocidal intent of the British Government not only in its refusal to accept the essential degree of fiscal responsibility, but also in the relief machinery itself and in the way it was allegedly designed to work. Whatever relief was made available to the hungry and the starving, whether in the form of employment or of soup or of a place in the workhouse, was ultimately designed to break the grip of the Irish farmer and cottier on his house and land, as a prelude to death at home or emigration and exile abroad. He was perfectly convinced that the consequences of British policy were not unintended but deliberately pursued, and he said so forcefully and repeatedly:

'When the new "Outdoor Relief" Act began to be applied, with its memorable quarter-acre clause, all this process went on with wonderful velocity, and millions of people were soon left landless and homeless. That they should be left landless and homeless was strictly in accordance with British policy; but then there was danger of the millions of outcasts becoming robbers and murderers. Accordingly, the next point was to clear the country of them and diminish the poor rates by *emigration*.'

Although the British Government did not directly promote mass emigration, Mitchel poured scorn on the idea that the huge exodus was voluntary in any meaningful sense. If landlords cleared estates by means of the quarter-acre clause and chased 'the human surplus from pillar to post', so that relief under the poor law 'becomes the national way of living, you may be sure there will be a deep and pervading anxiety to get away...'. At that point, asserted Mitchel, the hypocritical and sanctimonious 'exterminators' would 'say to the public, "Help us to indulge the wish of our poor brethren; you perceive they *want* to be off. God forbid *we* should ship them away, save with their cordial concurrence!"'

At first glance Mitchel's accusations may seem far-fetched, even wildly erroneous. And some of them surely were, such as the claim that before monies voted by parliament at the behest of Peel's government early in 1846 became available to relieve distress, 'many thousands had died of hunger'; or the claim, made in a diatribe against food exports in the midst of famine, that 'many a shipload [of Irish grain] was carried four times across the Irish Sea' to satisfy the injunctions of *laissez-faire.* But other charges contained a core of truth, or an important aspect of the truth, even if they were not wholly accurate. In this category were the murderous effects of allowing the grain harvest of 1846 to be exported, the refusal to make the cost of fighting the famine a United Kingdom charge, and the decree that from mid-1847 onwards Irish ratepayers (landlords and tenants) must bear all the expense of relieving the destitute. The harsh words which Mitchel had for Trevelyan do not seem to have been undeserved, even if the professional historian would choose different language. After all, in the closing paragraph of his 1848 book *The Irish crisis*, Trevelyan could be so insensitive as to describe the famine as 'a direct stroke of an all-wise and all-merciful Providence', one which laid bare 'the deep and inveterate root of social evil'; the famine, he declared, was 'the sharp but effectual remedy by which the cure is likely to be effected... God grant that the generation to which this opportunity has been offered may rightly perform its part'. As one historian has observed almost charitably, 'such a view was itself unconducive to substantial government intervention to relieve peasant suffering'. Nor is there much truth in the suggestion sometimes made by revisionist historians that the importance of Trevelyan, the assistant secretary of the Treasury, has been greatly exaggerated. Never was Treasury influence and control in more ascendancy.

Even John Mitchel's insistence on the perpetration of genocide becomes more understandable when certain crucial facts and their interrelationship are kept in mind. Among the lessons that 'the most frightful calamities' of 1846-47 had driven home, according to the incorrigibly blinkered Trevelyan, was that 'the proper business of a government is to enable private individuals of every rank and profession in life to carry on their several occupations with freedom and safety, and not itself to undertake the business of the landowner, merchant, moneylender, or any other function of social life'. Admittedly, the massive public works and the ubiquitous government-sponsored soup kitchens had violated the doctrinaire *laissez-faire* views thus espoused by Trevelyan, but that is precisely the point: they were gross violations which very recent experience, as interpreted by Trevelyan (and Whig ministers) in late 1847, had shown should never be repeated. And they were not, even though the greater part of famine mortality was yet to come.

As if to make amends for its misguided profligacy through the summer of 1847, Russell's Whig Government then moved to fix almost the entire fiscal burden on the Irish poor-law system. The 130 poor-law unions into which Ireland was divided were each self-contained raisers and spenders of their own tax revenue; the poorest unions in the country were to go it alone, their ratepayers sinking under the accumulating weight of the levies needed to support a growing mass of pauperism. It mattered not in the eyes of the British Government whether this weak fiscal structure was really capable of keeping mass death at bay. What mattered was the supposedly universal and timeless validity of a then-cherished economic doctrine. 'There is', declared Trevelyan in late 1847, 'only one way in which the relief of the destitute ever has been or ever will be conducted consistently with the general welfare, and that is by *making it a local charge*'. It was on this principle that British policy rested from mid-1847 onwards, with the result that, as Trevelyan himself said (and said proudly), 'The struggle now is to keep the poor off the rates'.

What we would consider serious defects of this tragically excessive reliance on the Irish poor-law system were not necessarily regarded as such by Trevelyan or Whig ministers. Certain key features of the Irish poor law, especially the notorious quarter-acre clause and the less well-known £4-rating provision, led directly to mass evictions, to the infamous clearances. British officials and Irish landlords mentally insulated themselves against the inhumanity and often murderous consequences of mass evictions by taking the view that clearances were now both inevitable and essential to Irish economic progress. The potato failure had simply deprived conacre tenants and cottiers of any future in their current status. 'The position occupied by these classes', Trevelyan insisted in *The Irish crisis*, 'is no longer tenable, and it is necessary for them to become substantial farmers or to live by the wages of their labour'. Although a towering mass of human misery lay behind the twin processes of clearance and consolidation, Trevelyan (and many others) could minimise the human tragedy and concentrate on the economic miracle in the making. Among the signs that 'we are advancing by sure steps toward the desired end', remarked Trevelyan laconically in *The Irish crisis*, was the prominent fact that 'the small holdings, which have become deserted owing to death or emigration or the mere inability of the holders to obtain a subsistence from them in the absence of the potato, have, to a considerable extent, been consolidated with the adjoining farms; and the middlemen, whose occupation depends on the existence of a numerous small tenantry, have begun to disappear'. Is it not remarkable that in this passage describing the huge disruption of clearance and consolidation, the whole question of agency is pleasantly evaded? Tenants are not dispossessed by anyone; rather, small holdings 'become deserted', and the reasons assigned for that do not include eviction. But whatever the reasons, the transformation is warmly applauded.

There is thus no cause to think that Trevelyan would have disagreed with the Kerry landlord who affirmed privately in October 1852 that 'the destruction of the potato is a blessing to Ireland'. This was the common view among the landed élite. Lord Lansdowne's agent W.S. Trench put the same point somewhat differently in September of the same year: 'Nothing but the successive failures of the potato...could have produced the emigration which will, I trust, give us room to become civilised'. But the connecting line that ran from the blight to mass evictions and mass emigration embraced the poor-law system imposed by Britain. As the economist Nassau Senior was told in 1852 by his brother, himself an Irish poor-law commissioner, 'The great instrument which is clearing Ireland is the poor law. It supplies both the motive and the means... It was passed for the purpose of relieving England and Scotland at the expense of Ireland; it will probably relieve Ireland at the expense of England and Scotland'.

British ministers could also regard with perfect equanimity yet another major consequence of the operation of the poor law during the famine. This was the severe strain which it placed on the solvency of many Irish landlords. The Irish landed élite was generally viewed hypercritically in British political circles. Indeed, in the British mythology of the famine the feckless, improvident and irresponsible Irish landlord was second in sinister importance only to the idling and duplicitous Irish pauper labourer. British officials traced many of the worst evils of the Irish economic and social system to what they considered the landlords' criminal neglect. For this reason, the poor rates which landlords in impoverished parts of the south and west found so crushing in the late 1840s served in Trevelyan's eyes the highest social and moral purposes. 'The principle of the poor law', he declared, 'is that rate after rate should be levied *for the preservation of life* until the landowners and farmers either enable the people to support themselves by honest industry or dispose of their property to those who can and will perform this indispensable duty.'

Thus it was a distinct gain when many Irish landlords were driven into bankruptcy by the burden of poor rates and other famine-related losses. Their insolvency was part of that wider opportunity provided by 'an all-wise and all-merciful Providence' which must now be seized. By making it much easier for the clamouring creditors of bankrupt or heavily indebted Irish landlords to move against them, British ministers aimed to confer on a backward Irish agricultural system the elixir or magical healing of British capital and enterprise. This was the acknowledged strategy behind the famous Incumbered Estates Act of 1849 and its abortive predecessor. How much importance the Whig Government attached to this legislation was signalled by Trevelyan in *The Irish crisis*: 'The fact is that the main hope of extrication from the slough of despond in which the small holders in the centre and west of Ireland are at present sunk is from the enterprise and capital and improved husbandry of the class of owners commonly known by the name of landlords'. Clearly, the landlords whom Trevelyan and the Whigs had in mind were not the current Irish landed élite, whose members he accused of relinquishing 'their position in rural society'.

What should we make of all this? First, it is now much easier to see why John Mitchel could plausibly accuse the British Government of genocide against the people of Ireland in the late 1840s, and why his indictment should have had such resonance at the popular level. The cost in human life of both what the government did and what it omitted to do was enormous. As to the bald charge of genocide, Mitchel was wrong. A.J.P. Taylor was right when he said of those who presided over British relief policy (Lord John Russell, Sir Charles Wood, and Trevelyan) that 'they were highly conscientious men, and their consciences never reproached them'. But an analytical survey of the means, ends, and results of British policy does not leave much scope for the persistent inclination of revisionist historians to adopt what we might call a forgive-and-forget attitude.

Why they would want to do this, or why they might have done this even unconsciously, is itself an interesting and somewhat perplexing question. Part of the explanation is no doubt that they have been disinclined to judge the British response to the Great Famine harshly when the recent governmental record of fighting famine around the world has left so much to be desired, even after striking advances in technology and communications. Another part of the explanation may well be the probably correct perception that even limited endorsement of the Mitchel indictment would give political aid and comfort to revolutionary Irish nationalists in our own time, whose version of this catastrophic episode in Irish history is a simplified rendition of Mitchel's. Still another reason may be related to the obvious fact that Mitchel wrote *The last conquest* with a determined propagandist purpose, and it was his view that became and long remained by far the dominant popular interpretation among Irish Catholics at home and abroad. Historians, however, are not in the business of echoing past propaganda or of endorsing the popular myths used to forge new nations. Revisionist historians have seen it as their special duty to explode such myths. But they must also seek a fuller understanding of the degree to which Mitchel's enormously effective propaganda corresponded to reality or illuminated it, and they cannot allow the political concerns of our own day to deflect them from this essential task.

Bibliography

Bourke, Austin, 'The Visitation of God'? The Potato and the Great Irish Famine (Dublin, 1993).

Bradshaw, Brendan, 'Nationalism and historical scholarship in modern Ireland' in Irish Historical Studies, xxvi, no. 104 (November 1989), 329-51.

Briggs, Asa and Susan Briggs (eds.), Cap and Bell: Punch's Chronicle of English History in the Making 1841-1861 (London, 1972).

Connell, K.H., The Population of Ireland 1750-1845 (Oxford, 1951).

Crawford, E. Margaret (ed.), Famine: the Irish Experience 900-1900 (Edinburgh, 1989).

Crowley, John, Mike Murphy and William J. Smyth, Atlas of the Great Irish Famine (Cork, 2012).

Curtis, L. Perry, Apes and Angels: the Irishman in Victorian Caricature (London, 1971).

Clarkson, Lesley A. and E. Margaret Crawford, Feast and Famine: Food and Nutrition in Ireland 1500-1920 (Oxford, 2001).

Edwards, R.D and T.D. Williams (eds.), The Great Famine: Studies in Irish History 1845-52 (Dublin, 1956).

Fitzpatrick, David, Irish Emigration, 1820-1921 (Dundalk, 1984).

Goodbody, Rob, A Suitable Channel: Quaker Relief in the Great Famine (Dublin, 1995).

Guinnane, Timothy, The Vanishing Irish: Households, Migration, and the Rural Economy in Ireland, 1850-1914 (Princeton, 1997).

Kerr, Donal A, The Catholic Church and the Famine (Dublin, 1996).

Kinealy, Christine, 'This great calamity': The Irish Famine, 1845-52 (Dublin, 1995).

Kinealy, Christine, 'A Death-Dealing Famine': The Great Hunger in Ireland (London, 1997).

Lowe, W.J., 'Policing Famine Ireland' Eire-Ireland, xxix, no.4 (Winter 1994), 47-67.

Lowe, W.J. and Elizabeth L. Malcolm, 'The Domestication of the Royal Irish Constabulary, 1836-1922', Irish Economic and Social History, xix (1992), 27-48.

McClaughlin, Trevor, Barefoot and Pregnant? Irish Famine orphans in Australia (Melbourne, 1991).

McClaughlin, Trevor (ed.), Irish Women in Colonial Australia (Sydney, 1998).

Ó Murchadha, Ciarán, The Great Famine: Ireland's Agony, 1845-1852 (London, 2012).

Mac Suibhne, Breandán, *The End of Outrage: Post-Famine Adjustment in Rural Ireland* (Oxford, 2017).

MacKay, Donald, *Flight from Famine: The Coming of the Irish to Canada* (Toronto, 1990).

Morash, Christopher and Richard Hayes (eds.), *Fearful Realities: New Perspectives on the Famine* (Dublin, 1996).

Ó Ciosin, Niall, 'Famine Memory and the Popular Representation of Scarcity', in Ian McBride (ed.) , *History and Memory in Modern Ireland* (Cambridge, 2001).

O'Gallagher, Marianne and Rose Dompierre (eds), *Eyewitness: Grosse Île 1847* (Quebec, 1995).

Ó Gráda, Cormac, *The Great Irish Famine* (London, 1989).

Ó Gráda, Cormac, *Ireland: A New Economic History 1780-1939* (Oxford, 1994).

Ó Gráda, Cormac, *Black '47 and Beyond: the Great Irish Famine in History, Economy, and Memory* (Princeton, 1999).

Ó Gráda, Cormac, *Famine: A Short History* (Princeton, 2009).

O'Sullivan, Patrick (ed.), *The Meaning of the Famine* (Leicester, 1996).

Poirtéir, Cathal (ed.), *The Great Irish Famine* (Cork, 1995).

Reid, Richard and Cheryl Mongan, *'A Decent Set of Girls': the Irish Famine orphans of the Thomas Arbuthnot 1849–1850* (Yass, 1996).

Robins, Joseph, *The Lost Children: a Study of Charity Children in Ireland 1700–1900* (Dublin, 1980).

Vaughan, W.E. and A.J. Fitzpatrick, *Irish Historical Statistics: Population, 1821-1971* (Dublin, 1978).

Woodham-Smith, Cecil, *The Great Hunger: Ireland 1845-1849* (London, 1962).

Walker, B.M., 'Villain, Victim or Prophet?: William Gregory and the Great Famine' , *Irish Historical Studies*, xxxviii, no.152 (Nov. 2013), 579-99.

Walker, B.M., 'Politicians, Elections and Catastrophe: The General Election of 1847', *Irish Political Studies* 22 (1) (2007), 1-34.